FIRST CERTIFICATE
GRAMMAR WORKBOOK

MICHAEL VINCE

Liz Chill

Victoria AEC

Hillingdon

Heinemann International
A division of Heinemann Educational Books Ltd
Halley Court, Jordan Hill, Oxford OX2 8EJ

OXFORD LONDON EDINBURGH
MELBOURNE SYDNEY AUCKLAND
SINGAPORE MADRID IBADAN
NAIROBI GABORONE HARARE
ATHENS BOLOGNA PARIS TOKYO
PORTSMOUTH (NH)

ISBN 0 435 28181 X (without answer key)

© Michael Vince 1989

First published 1989

ISBN 0 435 28185 2 (with answer key)

© Michael Vince 1990

First published 1990

Designed by Sue Vaudin

Cover photograph by Pictor International

Typeset by Tradespools Ltd, Frome, Somerset
Printed and bound in Great Britain by
Thomson Litho Ltd, East Kilbride, Scotland

91 92 93 94 95 10 9 8 7 6 5 4

CONTENTS

SECTION 1   GRAMMAR

UNIT 1   Articles (1)   6
Definite article; indefinite article; zero article

UNIT 2   Articles (2)   8
Further practice with articles

UNIT 3   Prepositions (1)   10
Prepositions of: movement, position and place;
purpose, cause, origin, instrument, common
problems

UNIT 4   Prepositions (2)   12
Further practice with prepositions

UNIT 5   Present time   14
Present Simple: position of adverbs; Present
Continuous: states and events; problems with
Simple and Continuous

UNIT 6   Present Perfect   15
Time concept; *for* and *since*; Present Perfect,
Simple and Continuous; contrasts with other
tenses

UNIT 7   Future time   17
Will and *shall*; future use of Present
Continuous; *going to*; Future Perfect; future
use of Present Simple; Future Continuous

UNIT 8   Past time   19
Past Simple; Past Continuous; *used to*; Past
Perfect; *would*; problems with past time

UNIT 9   Tense contrasts   20
Further practice with tenses

UNIT 10   Mixed tenses   22
Further practice with tenses

UNIT 11   First and Second Conditionals 23
What always happens; real condition; ability;
conditional ability; unreal condition; unreal
conditional ability; contrast of Conditionals 1
and 2; *unless*

**UNIT 12   Third Conditional and contrasts
                of First, Second and Third
                Conditionals   25**
Conditional about the past; conditional and
past ability; contrasts of First, Second and Third
Conditionals

**UNIT 13   Wishes and other
                hypotheticals   26**
Wishes about the present; wishes about the
past; wishes about ability; wishes about
annoying habits; *it's time* plus persons;
I'd rather plus persons

**UNIT 14   Time clauses and
                time words (1)   28**
Time clauses; time clauses which emphasise
completion; time words; *still, yet, already*

UNIT 15   Time words (2)   29
*At first, at last, in the end, at the end;
eventually, recently, lately, presently,
nowadays; first, second,* etc.; periods of time;
frequency

UNIT 16   Functions (1)   31
Identifying different functions

UNIT 17   Functions (2)   32
Eight useful areas

**UNIT 18   Certainty and uncertainty –
                Present Time   34**
May and *might; could; perhaps* and *possibly; is
bound to, is certain to; must* and *can't*

**UNIT 19   Certainty and uncertainty –
                Past Time   35**
May have and *might have; could have; is bound
to have; must have* and *can't have*

UNIT 20   Obligation – Present Time   36
Must and *have to; should* and *ought to; need*
and *need to; is to* and *are to*

UNIT 21   Obligation – Past Time   37
Must have to and *have got to; should* and
ought to; need to and *need; was to*

UNIT 22   Ability and permission   39
Present ability; future ability; past ability;
manage to; permission

UNIT 23   Passive (1)   40
Tense and forms; agent or no agent; transitive
and intransitive verbs

UNIT 24   Passive (2)   42
Get/have something done; reports; verbs with
two objects; other problems

UNIT 25   Reported speech (1)   43
Backshift or not? questions, commands and
explanations; reference words

UNIT 26   Reported speech (2)   45
Paraphrase; reporting words

UNIT 27   Comparison   46
Comparing with adjectives; problems with
formation of adjectives; comparing with
adverbs; spelling problems

UNIT 28   Relative pronouns   48
Which and *who; whose; what;* defining and
non-defining relative clauses; *whom;* leaving
out *who* and *which*

UNIT 29   Infinitive   49
Verbs followed by full infinitive; object and full
infinitive; bare infinitive without *to*

UNIT 30   Infinitive and *-ing* forms (1)   51
Verbs followed by *-ing* forms

UNIT 31   **Infinitive and *-ing* forms (2)**   52
Verbs followed by *to* or *-ing*; changes of meaning; verbs of perception

UNIT 32   **Phrasal verbs (1)**   54
Verbs with three parts

UNIT 33   **Phrasal verbs (2)**   55
Two parts, splittable

UNIT 34   **Phrasal verbs (3)**   57
Two parts, no object

UNIT 35   **Phrasal verbs (4)**   58
Two parts, object, unsplittable

UNIT 36   **Adverbs of degree**   60
So and *such*; *too* and *very*; *rather* and *quite*

UNIT 37   **Verbs and prepositions**   61
To; *of*; *with*; *for*; *on*; *in*; *about*

UNIT 38   **Prepositions (3)**   63
Prepositions following adjectives; prepositional phrases

UNIT 39   **Quantifiers**   64
All, each, every, both; *neither, none, not . . . either*; *much, many, little, few*

UNIT 40   **Punctuation**   66
Apostrophe; comma; colon and semi-colon; other punctuation: brackets, hyphen and speech marks

UNIT 41   **Pronunciation and spelling**   67
Same sounds with different spellings; spelling rules for common problems

SECTION 2   *VOCABULARY*

UNIT 42   **Travel, Transport and Tourism**   70

UNIT 43   **Shopping and Money**   71

UNIT 44   **Sport and Leisure**   73

UNIT 45   **House and Contents**   75

UNIT 46   **Work**   77

UNIT 47   **Food and Eating**   79

UNIT 48   **Health, Fitness and the Body**   81

UNIT 49   **Character, Appearance and Clothes**   83

UNIT 50   **Entertainment and the Arts**   85

UNIT 51   **Social and Environmental Issues**   86

UNIT 52   **Word Building (1)**   88

UNIT 53   **Word Building (2)**   90

UNIT 54   **Connectors**   92
Although, in spite of, despite; *as, since, because*; *in order to, so as to, so that*; *as if, as though*; *the (longer) . . ., the (better)*; *except for, apart from*; *while, whereas*

UNIT 55   **Discourse markers**   93
Ordering; adding and emphasising; summing up and giving opinions; giving examples; showing results; contrasting; concession; punctuation; formality

UNIT 56   **Singulars, plurals, countables and uncountables**   95
Common uncountables; irregular plurals; unchanging plurals; problems with countables and uncountables

Appendix   **Useful phrases**   96

ARTICLES (1)

1 *Definite article* **the**

a with things known or previously mentioned:
The money is on the table
(we know which money and which table)

b with things made specific by a defining word, phrase or clause:
The water here tastes strange
She's the woman who owns the house

c with adjectives to describe a class of people:
the rich the blind the poor the old

d with superlatives:
He's the richest person I know (But: *Most people are not rich*)

e with musical instruments when they are played:
She plays the piano

f with plural names of countries:
the Soviet Union the Netherlands the United States

g with names of ranges of mountains, rivers and oceans:
the Alps the Thames the Mediterranean

h with names of nationalities meaning 'the people generally':
the Italians are fond of opera
The English drink a lot of tea

i with unique objects:
the sun the moon

j with adjectives to mean 'things':
The imaginary is often deceptive
(= imaginary things)

k with one word which stands for a class of people or animals:
The dog is related to the wolf
The working man wants more leisure

2 *Indefinitive article* **a/an**

a with general reference:
*She has a bicycle (She has **the** bicycle* = the one we talked of)

b with *be, become, work as,* especially referring to jobs:
He became an actor She works as a computer programmer

c with words of time to express how often something happens:
It happens three times a day She earns £20,000 a year

d meaning *one:*
Bring me a beer please It's worth a thousand pounds

3 *Zero article*

a with countable and uncountable nouns to refer to a general class:
Pens last longer than pencils Water is the most refreshing drink

b with abstract ideas used generally:
Peace is a wonderful thing Beauty is only skin deep

c with names of seasons, times of day, meals, transport, illness and other idiomatic uses:
It is lovely here in summer (But: *I was there in the summer* = this year)
I got up at midday I had lunch and left
I went there by car (But: *I went there in a taxi) The use of the article depends on the preposition She was suffering from 'flu*

EXERCISES

Put *the, a/an* or nothing in each space.

1
1 They put all _____ money in _____ box and sent it to _____ appeal for _____ deaf and dumb.

2 She climbed _____ highest mountain in _____ world, in _____ Himalayas.

3 _____ man who lives in _____ flat next door is _____ musician.

4 He asked _____ waiter to bring _____ soft drink and _____ menu.

5 They had _____ best holiday they had ever had by _____ lake in _____ Switzerland.

6 _____ beauty of _____ scenery in _____ film I saw last night was fantastic.

7 By _____ training in _____ swimming-pool twice _____ day she became _____ champion.

8 I told _____ removal men to put _____ piano in _____ living-room.

9 _____ French drink _____ wine more than _____ English do.

10 He bought _____ boat and crossed _____ Atlantic for _____ bet.

2 Suddenly (1)_____ police car stopped outside (2)_____ gate, and (3)_____ tall policeman got out. He took (4)_____ careful look at (5)_____ house for (6)_____ moment, as if he was looking for (7)_____ someone or (8)_____ something, and came into (9)_____ garden. Suddenly (10)_____ enormous dog, which must have been hiding behind (11)_____ hedge, dashed out and bit (12)_____ policeman in (13)_____ leg. He gave (14)_____ yell of (15)_____ pain, and closed (16)_____ gate in (17)_____ hurry.

3
1 _____ first time I saw _____ octopus was in _____ Mediterranean.

2 She is _____ talented musician who can play _____ violin and conduct _____ orchestra.

3 _____ worst job I had was in _____ bakery, and I earned only £5 _____ week.

4 _____ tourist steamers on _____ Thames go from _____ Houses of Parliament to _____ Tower of London.

5 They have _____ cat which often has _____ fights with _____ dogs.

6 There's _____ school I know where _____ students who come late have to explain _____ reason to _____ head teacher.

7 _____ most depressing thing about _____ English winter is _____ thought that there will be _____ rain and _____ cold for _____ months.

8 _____ first man to land on _____ moon said: 'This is _____ small step for _____ man, but _____ giant step for _____ mankind'.

9 _____ nuclear accidents have made _____ most people worried about _____ nuclear power.

10 _____ peace and happiness of _____ millions of _____ people are impossible unless _____ man makes an effort to abolish _____ war.

4 (1)_____ problem of (2)_____ pollution has become one of (3)_____ most serious problems in (4)_____ modern world. (5)_____ modern city dweller now breathes in (6)_____ fumes of (7)_____ heavy traffic, and has to put up with (8)_____ noise which often causes damage to (9)_____ ears, besides forcing (10)_____ most people to live in a state of (11)_____ constant stress. However, it is not only in (12)_____ city that (13)_____ pollution is (14)_____ major problem. Even in (15)_____ apparent peace and quiet of (16)_____ countryside, (17)_____ danger from (18)_____ overuse of (19)_____ chemical fertilisers and (20)_____ pesticides had become (21)_____ cause for (22)_____ concern. (23)_____ authorities are aware of (24)_____ problem, but, as with (25)_____ industrial pollution, it is (26)_____ cost of reducing (27)_____ dangers which often prevents (28)_____ action being taken.

ARTICLES (2)

Refer back to Unit 1 for guidance

1 Put *the, a/an* or nothing in each space.

Our guided tour of ___(1)___ world will be ___(2)___ most exciting adventure of your life. It includes ___(3)___ visit to ___(4)___ United States, where you spend ___(5)___ week in ___(6)___ New York; ___(7)___ visit to ___(8)___ Wild West and to ___(9)___ Disneyland; and finally four days on ___(10)___ shores of ___(11)___ Pacific in ___(12)___ San Francisco. From there you fly to ___(13)___ Japan, where there are ___(14)___ trips to ___(15)___ Mount Fuji and ___(16)___ sights of ___(17)___ Tokyo. From ___(18)___ Japan you go on to ___(19)___ China, where you spend ___(20)___ exciting week visiting ___(21)___ ancient cities of ___(22)___ Peking and ___(23)___ Shanghai. Then ___(24)___ tour continues with ___(25)___ stops in all ___(26)___ most exotic places of ___(27)___ Far East – ___(28)___ Hong Kong, ___(29)___ Philippines, ___(30)___ Java, ___(31)___ Bangkok, and finally on to ___(32)___ India. There you will see ___(33)___ Taj Mahal, and walk beside ___(34)___ Ganges. Next stop is ___(35)___ Egypt – ___(36)___ Cairo and ___(37)___ Pyramids, followed by ___(38)___ stops in ___(39)___ Athens, where you climb to ___(40)___ Acropolis; ___(41)___ Rome, where you will visit ___(42)___ Vatican; and ___(43)___ Paris, which you will see from ___(44)___ top of ___(45)___ Eiffel Tower. When you touch down again at ___(46)___ Heathrow Airport, you will be ___(47)___ seasoned traveller.

2 Correct all the incorrect uses of *the, a/an* in these sentences.

1 I not only play piano, but am best violinist in the my class.
2 The friend of my brother's, a Mr Jameson, arrived at the house.
3 The day I lost my sunglasses was the bad day for me.
4 The Shakespeare is one of most famous English writers.
5 The most people in my town like the icecream made there.
6 First time I went to the theatre I saw the *Hamlet*.

7 I like the tennis most of all; it's the relaxing sport.
8 Long time ago I met the owner of that hotel.
9 Is that a girl I met at a party at John's house last week?
10 War between French and English lasted for hundred years.

3 For each sentence in the pair, choose the most suitable ending given, a or b, depending on whether the meaning is general, or definite.

1 Books left in the rain _____
2 The books left in the rain _____
  a get wet.
  b got wet.
3 He knew that history _____
4 He knew that the history _____
  a was a difficult subject.
  b of the town was interesting.
5 She valued the love _____
6 She valued love _____
  a most of all.
  b her grandmother gave her.
7 He thought that man _____
8 He thought that the man _____
  a looked like his old teacher.
  b had an uncertain future.
9 She believed that wisdom _____
10 She believed that the wisdom _____
  a was difficult to come by.
  b of the East was superior.
11 He was the last _____
12 He was last _____
  a person to arrive.
  b to arrive.
13 People without passports _____
14 The people without passports _____
  a had to go to the police.
  b have no interest in travel.
15 They agreed that the America _____
16 They agreed that America _____
  a of today was different.
  b was different.
17 She drank a glass of wine _____
18 She drank a glass of the wine _____
  a her husband had brought.
  b and became more talkative.
19 He arrived on Monday _____
20 He arrived on the Monday _____
  a and we got married.
  b we got married.

4 Put *the*, *a/an* or nothing in each space.

Mr Burton was (1)_____ first French teacher I had, and he was also (2)_____ most extraordinary person in (3)_____ school. He always wore (4)_____ dirty sports jacket with (5)_____ very large handkerchief in (6)_____ top pocket. He was always (7)_____ last to arrive in (8)_____ room, usually about ten minutes after (9)_____ rest of (10)_____ school had begun (11)_____ lessons. He was (12)_____ fat, slow person with (13)_____ very loud voice, who seemed to spend most of (14)_____ lesson talking to himself. (15)_____ best part of (16)_____ lesson was when he fell asleep, which usually happened about once (17)_____ week. Once we managed to go out of (18)_____ room quietly, and left him asleep at (19)_____ desk until (20)_____ next class arrived.

5 Put *the*, *a/an* or nothing in each space.

1 _____ water is _____ healthiest drink in _____ most parts of _____ world.
2 _____ first people who live on _____ moon will be short of _____ water.
3 Take _____ first road on _____ left and _____ house is opposite _____ church.
4 In _____ future I expect _____ people will live under _____ sea.
5 I think _____ light needs changing in _____ bathroom.
6 _____ best thing about _____ love is _____ way it changes people.
7 I went there in _____ taxi because I had _____ headache.
8 _____ lot of _____ people in my area mistrust _____ police.
9 _____ first time I went to _____ dance I learned _____ waltz.
10 _____ unhappiness is often _____ result of _____ loneliness.

6 Put *the*, *a/an* or nothing in each space.

1 _____ Nelson's Column is in _____ Trafalgar Square in _____ London.
2 _____ British Airways is one of _____ airlines who use _____ Concorde.

3 _____ discovery of _____ atomic power has proved _____ unfortunate.
4 _____ ancient Greeks had _____ wide knowledge of _____ mathematics.
5 _____ empty house needs _____ Electroglow fire.
6 _____ number two is running _____ much faster than _____ number four.
7 _____ spring in _____ Greek Islands can be rather chilly.
8 _____ beer you're drinking comes from _____ German grocer's opposite.
9 _____ stitch in _____ time saves _____ nine.
10 _____ last question is usually _____ easiest.

UNIT 3

PREPOSITIONS (1)

Units 4, 14, 15, 38, 39 also include practice with prepositions

Prepositions generally cover a number of meanings and uses, so it is very important to think about the context of use.

1 Movement

With verbs of movement, e.g. *come, go, run, fall*, etc. the following prepositions generally indicate the direction involved.

He ran **up** the stairs
We walked **around** the park
I drove **towards** the hills
He climbed **through** the window
I ran **behind** the tree
They ran **across** the road
It rolled **down** the hill
She ran **from** the room
She came **into** the room
They fell **out (of)** the window
She fell **off** the horse
He climbed **over** the fence
He walked **past** the church
She drove **onto** the pavement
I strolled **along** the sea-front
They walked **to** the cinema

2 Position and Place

He lives **behind** that church
Park **in front of** the house
He was standing **beside** the window
They hung the holly **above** the door
It's **on top of** the fridge
I left the money **under** the clock
She works **near** the centre
It's **between** Leeds and Bradford
She lives **in** the city centre
Turn **before** the traffic lights
It's **after** that building
She sat **by** the exit
I put the carpet **over** the stain
It's **underneath** that book
The oil must be **below** this mark
The house is **among** those trees
He sat **on** the sofa
I saw them **at** the cinema

Some of the prepositions in Section 1 (*around, out of, over, behind, past, across, down, along*) can also be used to define position (= where no movement is involved).

He lives across the road
Her office is along that corridor

3 Other uses

(See also Units 14, 15, 38, 39)

Purpose: Everything I did, I did **for** you
            I gave them a present **out of** pity
(Cause):   **Because of** the rain, the match was cancelled
            Most of the villagers died **from** starvation
Origin: He comes **from** Italy
Instrument: I went to work **by** bus
            He opened the can **with** a knife

4 Common problems

a *to* can only be used with verbs of movement:
   I went to school   I arrived at school

b *at* is used with places, *in* is used with names of cities and countries:
   We arrived in Athens   We landed at Athens Airport

c Expressions describing forms of transport, e.g. *by bus*, are generalised. If a personal form of transport is involved, *in* or *on* are used:
   I went there by car   I went there in her car
   I went there by boat   I went there on her boat
   I went there in a plane   (i.e. with the article.)

d usually we get *on* or *off* a bus, train, plane, bicycle, horse, etc.
   (the vehicle is higher than we are)
   but we get *in (to)* and *out (of)* a car
   (the vehicle is lower than we are)

e *into* and *onto* involve movement, and follow the use of *to*

f *leave* is followed by *for* if a destination is involved:
   He left for Manchester ten minutes ago

EXERCISES

1 Put *on, in, at, to* or nothing in each space.

1 They decided to go _____ France _____ John's car.
2 We arrived _____ London Airport and stayed _____ a hotel.
3 I met her _____ the cinema while we were _____ a queue for tickets.
4 The exercise _____ page 14 is rather easy.
5 I arrived _____ the office and put the papers _____ the table.
6 I went _____ the theatre last night, and sat _____ a good seat.
7 When I got _____ the end of the road, I parked _____ a side turning.
8 I put the vegetables _____ the sink, and left _____ the kitchen.
9 I sat _____ the table and waited until he put the food _____ my plate.
10 The wine _____ that restaurant is rather expensive.

2 Put a suitable preposition in each space (note: a preposition may be a single word, or consist of more than one word).

1 They live _____ the supermarket and the greengrocer's.
2 He stayed _____ a small island which was exactly _____ the town.
3 Their summer house is up on the mountain just _____ this village.
4 The car _____ them didn't stop and it damaged their boot door.
5 In the winter I wear a thick vest _____ my shirt to keep warm.
6 I waited for ages in the queue because the man _____ me took so long.
7 There was a policeman standing _____ the entrance when I arrived.
8 She hid _____ the door and jumped out as he came in.
9 I put the present _____ the bookcase so little Jim couldn't reach it.
10 When I'm _____ a horse I always wish I could get _____.

3 Put a suitable preposition of movement in each space.

1 The cat ran _____ the road so quickly that the car missed it.
2 We drove _____ some lovely scenery on our way to the sea.
3 The last time I swam _____ the island I did it in half an hour.

4 As I rode _____ the corner, my bike slipped on the wet road.
5 I could see him coming _____ the road towards me.
6 Although there was a fence in the way, the dog jumped _____ it.
7 She walked _____ the trees and came at last to an open field.
8 He walked _____ his old friend without saying a word.
9 She went _____ the shop without paying for the coffee.
10 They walked _____ and _____ for hours trying to keep warm.

UNIT 4
PREPOSITIONS (2)

Note: a preposition may be a single word, or may be made up of more than one word.

1 Put a suitable preposition in each space.

1 Which village is she staying _____?
2 What a big hole he must have fallen _____!
3 This town is just impossible to live _____.
4 The road she ran _____ is very dangerous indeed.
5 This cheese is famous all the world _____.
6 The building which we have just driven _____ is the oldest in town.
7 Where exactly are you driving _____?
8 Which bus is she travelling _____?
9 The next town they arrived _____ was even smaller than the one before.
10 What a difficult place to get _____!
11 The path was far too steep to ride _____.
12 The area they travelled _____ was full of dangerous bandits.
13 The old monastery was very difficult to get _____.
14 What he was hiding _____ turned out to be a long black curtain.
15 The lamp they were standing _____ suddenly fell onto them.

2 Choose the correct preposition in each sentence.

1 They stayed for a month *in/on* a small island.
2 He arrived *in/at* school completely soaked to the skin.
3 The old man was murdered *with/by* a rusty knife.
4 I went to the match *in/by* my car.
5 They looked at themselves *in/on* the mirror.
6 The church is up the hill just *above/over* the castle.
7 She looked back and saw the road stretching *behind/in front of* her.
8 He lifted up the stone and found the box *on top/underneath*.
9 I spent an enjoyable week *in/at* Oxford.
10 She went *at/to* London University for three years.
11 She left her umbrella *to/at* the door.
12 I first saw her sitting *at/in* the cinema.
13 When they were *in/into* the room, they sat down.
14 He isn't quite so ill, but he's still *in/at* hospital.
15 The car went round a corner, the door opened, and she fell *off/out*.

3 Find the error in each sentence and correct it.

1 I travelled all round France with my car.
2 I reached to the station in time to catch the train.
3 We arrived in London Airport and took a bus to Reading.
4 There was an odd looking woman in front me in the queue.
5 The new supermarket is exactly opposite to the church.
6 The field with the mushrooms in it is just under the village.
7 She walked into the wood and was soon lost between the trees.
8 She stopped in the door and shook me by the hand.
9 Behind of the castle is a shop which is worth going into.
10 While he was walking over the street he was hit by a motorbike.
11 The house I have just moved into is just around of the corner.
12 Go on this road as far as the corner, and the cinema is opposite.
13 I couldn't get through the fence because it was too high.
14 They arrived towards the house, and stopped outside.
15 You drive down that road, and then turn to the right at the end.

4 Put a suitable preposition in each space.

All night the army remained (1)_____ its camp, the exhausted soldiers sitting (2)_____ their fires and the two generals arguing (3)_____ their tent. They were (4)_____ a plain with mountains all (5)_____ them. If they marched (6)_____ the main road, then Carlos and his army would come (7)_____ from the rocks and trap them (8)_____ the narrow pass. If they waited for General Van Stock to come (9)_____ their rescue, (and for all they knew, he was still (10)_____ the other side (11)_____ the mountains) they would not arrive (12)_____ Vilia in time. (13)_____ them, they could see other fires (14)_____ the darkness. The generals walked (15)_____ and (16)_____, smoking and talking. Suddenly they heard a shot right (17)_____ the tent, and an old man wrapped (18)_____ a cloak came rushing (19)_____ and fell (20)_____ their feet.

5 Choose the most suitable verb in each sentence.

1 The little girl passed/ran across the road without looking.
2 She kissed him and then walked/left out of the room.
3 I didn't go to/attend university but I learned a lot about life.
4 Go down this way and stop/continue at the end of the street.
5 They put/took the money into the box for safety.
6 Last summer when I went to/arrived at Paris I stayed with friends.
7 When I looked out of the window I saw someone coming/going towards me.
8 He stood/left by the door so as to avoid the crowd at the bar.
9 The train passed/stopped through the desert during the night.
10 The man in front of her kept following/annoying her.
11 Sue fell/climbed on the floor when she lost her balance.
12 I drove/left my car at the car-park.
13 He stood/hid between the trees at the bottom of the garden.
14 They lived/crossed on the other side of town.
15 She walked/looked across the wide stretch of blue sea.

6 Put a suitable preposition in each space. (There may be more than one correct answer.)

1 She crossed the room and stood _____ his side for a moment.
2 Just _____ the first houses of the town, there was a large factory.
3 He took a cigarette _____ his pocket and put it _____ her lips.
4 They stopped on the way _____ a small shop selling sandwiches.
5 The last company I worked _____ was probably the best.
6 Come on _____! The water's fine!
7 I wish you were here with me _____ Spain.
8 Suddenly there was a knock _____ the front door.
9 He could see a small village just _____ the border.
10 Maria was born _____ Crete, which is an island _____ Greece.
11 There were only two people _____ the queue, so I didn't wait long.
12 At the last fence the horse fell, trapping the jockey _____ it.
13 The football fans ran _____ the town shouting and breaking windows.
14 She drove the motorbike _____ the garage and got _____.
15 Bye! I'll see you _____ school tomorrow.

PRESENT TIME

1 Present Simple
  a habitual actions:
    I arrive at 8 every day (with 'events': see Point 4 below)
  b unrestricted in time:
    He lives in Chelsea (with 'states')
  c eternal truths:
    The earth goes around the sun

2 Position of adverbs
I usually arrive at 8 also: *often, sometimes, occasionally, rarely, never*
They are usually late.

3 Present Continuous
The following meanings are common; they may depend on the verb used.
  a the action is temporary:
    I'm washing my face
  b the action is unfinished:
    I'm reading 'War and Peace'
  c the action is repeated:
    I'm taking French lessons

    Two other meanings are also possible:
  d the action is repeated but within limits:
    Whenever I go there it's raining
  e the repeated action is an annoying habit:
    He's always coming late

4 States and events
The use of verbs can be divided into state and event:

States: e.g. *live, be, have* do not occur at only one time, but extend without a beginning and end.
Events: e.g. *arrive, cook, go* are limited actions which begin and end.

Using the Present Continuous makes an event seem longer, e.g. *I'm cooking*, but makes a state seem temporary, e.g. *I'm living in Chelsea*.
The difference between state and event also explains the two uses of *remember*.
    I remembered to do it = event
    I remember doing it = state

5 Problems with Simple and Continuous
  a verbs normally not in the Continuous form: *smell, hear, taste, think, believe, forget, know, understand, suppose, be, contain, have, own, matter, cost, depend*
  b some verbs have different meanings in Simple and Continuous:
    I can feel something moving
    I feel ill/I'm feeling ill (both possible)
    I'm having a party (an 'event')
    You are being silly (an 'event')
    I'm thinking of leaving
    (= considering)
    I'm seeing her tonight
    (= meeting)

EXERCISES
1 Write the *-ing* form of the following verbs. When you have checked your answers, write spelling rules for these verbs.

1 come	6 run	11 hide
2 write	7 find	12 think
3 swim	8 put	13 feel
4 decide	9 choose	14 do
5 like	10 fit	15 have

2 Put the verbs in brackets into the correct Present tense form.

  1 Henry usually (come) to visit me on Sunday.
  2 She (stand) at the end of the path waiting for you.
  3 I (hate) having to go out in the rain.
  4 I (think) of selling this car and buying a smaller one.
  5 While our house is being built we (stay) with John's parents.
  6 I (see) what you (mean) but I (not agree).
  7 I'm sorry but I can't talk now because I (cook).
  8 Oh not again! You always (lose) your front door keys.
  9 You always (hurt) the one you (love).
  10 You (not think) that you (be) rather silly?
  11 Time to get up! The sun (rise).
  12 I'm afraid I (lose) patience with you.
  13 I can't quite make it out, but he (write) something on the wall.
  14 Who this suitcase (belong) to?
  15 These boxes always (contain) the same things.

PRESENT PERFECT

3 Correct the errors in these sentences. (Some sentences have no errors.)

1 He does his homework at the moment.
2 He's having a cold all the time.
3 They're having a discussion about it next week.
4 I hope you are enjoying yourselves.
5 I am loving her very much.
6 She always is reading that silly comic.
7 I think of leaving here all the time.
8 Are you seeing them this afternoon?
9 Once a fortnight he is going for a long walk in the country.
10 I am feeling something round at the bottom of the box.
11 What do you do at the moment?
12 She is taking that medicine twice a day.
13 They really love what they are doing.
14 Are you believing in ghosts?
15 Look out! The shelf falls down!

4 Choose the most suitable verb form in each sentence.

1 When you can't sleep, what *do you think/ are you thinking* about?
2 *Do you ever cook/Are you ever cooking* early in the morning?
3 *Are you reading/Do you read* newspapers?
4 What *are you talking about/do you talk about* in the evenings?
5 How often exactly *do they have/are they having* parties?
6 What *does he see/is he seeing* in her?

1 *Time concept*

a with state verbs, a state lasting until now:
I've known her since 1984
b with event verbs, an indefinite event in the past (no time given):
Yes, I've eaten lunch
c with event verbs, a repeated event, like a habit, until now:
She's eaten lunch here for twenty years
d with verbs which show that the result of an action is still 'present':
He has broken his leg (that's why it's in plaster)

2 *Use of **for** and **since***

a *for* refers to a period of time:
I've known her for ten years
b *since* refers to a moment in time in the past:
I've known her since the conference
Note: this 'moment' may be a date, e.g. *1980*, an event, e.g. *the dance*, or a clause, e.g. *I've known her since I went to Italy.*

3 *Present Perfect Simple and Present Perfect Continuous*

a The Present Perfect Simple often indicates a completed action, especially if numbers are mentioned:
I've written ten letters this morning
I've been writing letters this morning has less sense of achievement.
This often depends on the verb used:
I've been reading that book = incomplete
I've read that book = complete
b Although the Present Perfect Continuous may suggest a temporary activity with state uses of verbs, the difference is small. The following two sentences both mean much the same.
How long have you lived here?
How long have you been living here?
c The Present Perfect Continuous suggests strong recent connection with the activity:
I've been waiting for hours (and I'm still standing here)
or describes an activity only recently completed:
I've been watching television i.e. that's finished now.

4 *Contrasts with other tenses*
   a with Present tenses:
      I have been here for a long time
      describes a period until now.
      I am here
      describes only this moment.
   b with Past tenses:
      How long did you live there?
      describes a completed period.
      How long have you lived here?
      describes an incomplete period because
      you live here now.
      Compare: *He has painted some lovely*
                portraits (he is alive)
                He painted some lovely
                portraits (he is dead, or no
                longer paints)

EXERCISES

1 Choose the most suitable tense in each
   sentence.

   1 *I am here/have been here* since eight
      o'clock.
   2 *I have stopped/have been stopping*
      worrying about it.
   3 *I never went/have never been* to Paris in my
      life.
   4 *I have been thinking/thought* about you a
      lot lately.
   5 *I've known/know* her for a long time.
   6 *I've done it/did it* two weeks ago.
   7 *I've made up/been making up* my mind at
      last.
   8 *I've told/been telling* you that twice before.
   9 *I like/have liked* you much more than I used
      to.
   10 What was that noise? What *has happened/
      has been happening*?
   11 What do you think *caused/has caused* the
      last war?
   12 What exactly have you *done/been doing* all
      this time?
   13 When *did you have/have you had* the baby?
   14 What's the matter? Why *have we stopped/
      did we stop*?
   15 *I saw/have seen* this film before.

2 Rewrite each sentence without changing the
   meaning beginning as given.

   1 I last saw him in 1968.
      I haven't _____
   2 This is the first time I have been to the
      opera.
      I haven't _____
   3 It's ages since I read a good book.
      I haven't _____
   4 I started waiting for you at six.
      I've _____
   5 That planet is unvisited by man.
      Man _____
   6 The last time I went there was eight years
      ago.
      I haven't _____
   7 Five of the letters are already complete.
      I've _____
   8 He appears to have fallen into the river.
      It seems that _____
   9 The match is still going on.
      The match has _____
   10 That was the last time I spoke to her.
      Since then _____

3 Complete each sentence, using the verb given,
   in either Present Perfect Simple, or Present
   Perfect Continuous.

   1 How long have you (learn) _____ English?
   2 Have you ever (eat) _____ lobster?
   3 Lately I (think) _____ of moving.
   4 Hasn't she (decide) _____ what to do yet?
   5 How much you (write) _____ so far today?
   6 Why she (cry) _____ ?
   7 Who you (invite) _____ to the party?
   8 Sorry I'm late. I (feel) _____ ill.

FUTURE TIME

(See also Units 11, 14, 15, 16)

1 *Uses of **will** and **shall***
  a *will* has many functional uses (see Units 16, 17) which are not exactly future time references, e.g. *I'll carry it for you* = Offer
  b *will* as future time reference is generally a prediction:
   I think it'll rain tomorrow
   Soon people will live on the moon
  c the use of *shall* with *I/we* is thought of as correct, but is not essential. *Shall* also has functional uses, e.g. *Shall I do it?* = Offer
  d both *will* and *shall* when stressed have the meaning of 'I insist on'.
  e in everyday speech the contractions *I'll, you'll*, etc. are more common.

2 *Future use of Present Continuous*
  a very common in making social arrangements:
   What are you doing on Saturday?
   I'm having a party
  b tends to refer to personal matters:
   I'm retiring next year = this is my personal arrangement
  c refers to a fixed arrangement, often a written one:
   My mother-in-law is coming to stay with us

3 *Going to*
  a refers to an intention or plan:
   What are you going to do this morning?
  b refers to the result of a cause which is present:
   Look out! That tree is going to fall down
   She is going to have a baby
  c although *going to* could be used in most examples in 2, it does suggest what the speaker wishes to do:
   I'm going to retire next year – if I can
   I'm going to have a party – some time soon perhaps

4 *Future Perfect*
  a This combines the meaning of the Present Perfect with that of the predictive future.
   Next year, we'll have been married fifteen years
   = when it is next year, we can say *'We have been married . . .'*; but this is still in the future.
  b This tense is commonly used with *by*, meaning 'some time before':
   By 10 o'clock, I'll have finished.
   = I'll finish some time before ten, and no later.

5 *Future use of Present Simple*
  more impersonal than the future use of the Present Continuous:
  The train leaves at 8
  I retire next year
  In both cases, the decision has been made by someone else.

6 *Future Continuous*
  The most common use transfers a period of time to the future:
  I'm lying on the beach
  This time next week, I'll be lying on the beach.

EXERCISES

1 Which of these sentences have correct uses of future time expressions?

1 I will have a party on Saturday.
2 The train is going to leave at 8.
3 This time next month I will live in my new house.
4 That car is going to crash into us.
5 I'm seeing him at 6 tomorrow.
6 I think it's raining tomorrow.
7 I'm going to stay with friends.
8 There won't be any food left.
9 On June 4th they'll be married for ten years.
10 OK, bye, I'm going to see you tomorrow.
11 They will go to France this summer for their holidays.
12 It's going to be a nice day tomorrow.
13 I think he's becoming president at the next election.
14 According to my diary, at 10 tomorrow I'm going to have a meeting.
15 What are you going to do about it?

2 Put the verbs in brackets into the most suitable future time form.

1 According to the timetable, the plane (take off) at 4.45.
2 It's a good film, isn't it. What do you think (happen) in the end?
3 They (build) our new house by the end of the year.
4 I (buy) a new car if I can sell the old one.
5 Oh dear, we've missed the boat. What we (do) now?
6 Sorry, I can't come. I (have) lunch with an old friend that day.
7 Look at those black clouds. I think it (rain).
8 She says she (phone) us tomorrow.
9 It seems that she (have) the baby any minute!
10 What time the sun (rise) tomorrow?
11 While you are travelling to work in the rain, I (sunbathe) in Spain!
12 I don't think they ever (find) the real murderer.
13 Don't worry. Someone (be) there at the airport to meet you.
14 Well, who (tell) him? You or me?
15 You (swim)? Or you (lie) on the beach all day?

3 Reply to each of these questions or statements using a suitable future time form, and using the cues given.

1 Would you like to come to the cinema with me tonight?
   Sorry, I/go/party
2 What have you got planned for this summer?
   We/stay/friends/Italy
3 Well, time to go. Bye.
   Bye. I/call/you tomorrow
4 Why don't we go there at about 11.30?
   No, that's too late. They/finish/eating by then
5 When are you going to start back at university?
   The new term start/Wednesday
6 Shall I come round at about 8?
   No, come later, we/eat/then

PAST TIME

1 Past Simple
a for past habitual actions:
   I usually left at 6
b for events in a narrative:
   Suddenly the telephone rang

2 Past Continuous
a for an extended action contrasted with a sudden event:
   While I was having a bath, the telephone rang
b to show that a past action is incomplete:
   I was painting the kitchen for a while
   Compare with:
   I painted the kitchen (= I finished it)
c to show that an action did not last:
   I was thinking of changing my job, but I decided against it
d to describe an annoying habit:
   He was always losing his keys

3 Used to
(Note: this only exists in the Past tense)
a to describe past habitual actions (can be states or events):
   When I lived there, I used to walk to work every day
b Past Simple could replace *used to*:
   When I lived there, I walked to work every day

4 Past Perfect/Past Perfect Continuous
a to show that one past event happened before another past event:
   When John arrived, they had all left
   They felt ill because they had been eating all evening
b this can also be shown by using *before/after*:
   John arrived after they had all left
c in reported speech, to report Past Simple or Present Perfect.
   He told me they had left
   He said, 'they have left'/He said, 'they left'

5 Would
Would is used to describe past habitual actions, generally in written texts, often of a literary kind, especially reminiscences (only event verbs).
Then everyone would open their presents, and we would all sing
It is advisable not to use this form in speech.

6 Problems with past time
The Past Continuous is not usually used to describe habitual actions. However, if the action is temporary, it may be used, especially if it supplies descriptive detail.
For the rest of the day, everyone was madly searching for the cat

EXERCISES

1 Find the errors in each sentence and correct them. (Some sentences are correct!)

   1 When I was a student, I was studying hard every day.
   2 I had lived in France once, but I haven't been there for ages.
   3 I was knowing what he was meaning but I was saying nothing.
   4 While I had eaten lunch, I was listening to the radio.
   5 Every day he was eating exactly the same things for breakfast.
   6 When we got there the film already finished.
   7 As I was getting into the lift, someone was speaking to me.
   8 I read a lot at one time but I don't use to any more.
   9 The last time I drank whisky I felt ill.
   10 There used to be a tree there, but someone had cut it down.
   11 I could see that he cried and I asked him what had happened.
   12 Why was she deciding to buy such a large house?
   13 The last thing I was hearing was the sound of the bells.
   14 When we had arrived, no-one had been there to meet us.
   15 What exactly were you doing after the policeman arrived?

2 Put the verb in brackets in a suitable Past time form.

   1 When I (live) in Bristol, I (go) to the theatre every week.
   2 While I (speak) on the phone, someone (come) to the door.
   3 I (get) there by 6, but he already (sell) the car to someone else.
   4 She (study) French and (give) French lessons at the same time!
   5 The problem is, why he (steal) the money?
   6 It seemed that someone (take) the cheque while she (sign) the papers.
   7 What he (say) when you (interrupt) him? He (get) angry?

TENSE CONTRASTS

8 At the time the earthquake (strike), I (write) a letter.
9 They (buy) that house because they (have) no choice.
10 The telephone call (annoy) me because I (try) to go to sleep.
11 Sophia (smile) when I (ask) her to dance.
12 He (pay) by cheque because someone (steal) his wallet.
13 Who she (talk) to when you (see) her for the first time?
14 How much a newspaper (cost) before they (put) up the price?
15 He (phone) her twice a day, but he doesn't do it so much now.

3 Put the verb in brackets in a suitable Past time form.

One day last summer as I (¹take) a walk, I (²notice) a small dog which (³bark) loudly in the middle of the road. I (⁴suppose) that someone (⁵lose) it, and so I (⁶pick) it up and (⁷take) it home. My children (⁸enjoy) looking after it, because they never (⁹have) a pet before. They (¹⁰take) it for a walk every morning, and they always (¹¹ask) me to let them keep it. But I (¹²try) to find the dog's owner ever since the day I (¹³find) it. That same day I (¹⁴put) an advertisement in the local paper, but so far no-one (¹⁵claim) the dog. Then suddenly one day while the children (¹⁶play) with the dog in the front garden, an old lady (¹⁷shout) at them, 'That's my dog! Here, Lucy!'. The dog (¹⁸run) to her, wagging its tail. Apparently she (¹⁹go) away on holiday with the dog, and somehow it (²⁰make) its way home from Scotland, more than 100 miles!

1 Put the verbs in brackets in the most suitable forms (including *going to/used to*)

1 I (not eat) such a delicious pizza since I (be) in Naples.
2 You (do) anything on Sunday? I (think) of having a party.
3 I'm sorry I (lock) the door. I (not realise) you (not leave).
4 I (not know) that you (live) in West Africa when I (be) there.
5 While they (argue) in the cafeteria, the train (leave).
6 The manager (decide) what (happen) in this office.
7 The last time I (go) to a cricket match it (rain).
8 You (go) to the new film on at the Odeon yet?
9 Someone (see) me leaving so I (hide) in the shadows.
10 When the policeman (fire) his gun, everyone (run).
11 I (look) for that pen ever since you (be) here last!
12 Oh, sorry, I (think) you (go).
13 By the end of next month, the sales (finish).
14 At the moment I (have) the feeling that the heating (not work).
15 The last time I (see) her she (just get) married.

2 Put the verbs in brackets in the most suitable forms.

While I (¹wait) for the last train to arrive, I (²walk) around the station. Some other unfortunate passengers who, like me, (³miss) the 11.30, (⁴sit) on benches half asleep. I (⁵sit) down next to an elderly man who (⁶offer) me a cigarette. 'You (⁷wait) for the 11.58?' he (⁸ask) me. 'I (⁹expect) it (¹⁰arrive) late as usual.' He (¹¹tell) me that he (¹²always catch) the last train from Basildon. 'Still, my daughter (¹³wait) for me at the station when I get there. She (¹⁴always collect) me. I (¹⁵try) to persuade her for years to let me walk home, but she says she (¹⁶enjoy) the trip.

3 Simple or Continuous?
Choose the most suitable verb form in each sentence.

1 *I have tried/been trying* to contact you ever since September.
2 What *was she saying/did she say* when you asked her?
3 What *do you think/are you thinking* about the new manager?

4 What *takes/is taking* you so long! Hurry up!
5 I *leave/am leaving* in the morning. *Do you come/Are you coming* too?
6 Lately he *has been considering/considered* a new offer from the firm.
7 That was lovely! But *I've eaten/been eating* far too much!
8 They*'ve been/were absent* very often lately.
9 Who *was talking/talked* to you last night when I *saw/was seeing* you?
10 According to the newspaper, the concert *is starting/starts* at 8.
11 *I've seen/been seeing* that film at least twice before.
12 I'm an architect. How about you? What *do you do/are you doing* exactly?
13 She *passed/was passing* her test but *isn't driving/doesn't drive* much.
14 I *won't work/won't be working* that afternoon, so come then.
15 They *met/were meeting* him while they *were flying/flew* to Canada.
16 I *have stayed/have been staying* in a hotel for the time being.

4 Put the verbs in brackets in the most suitable forms.

1 The last time I (eat) fish, I (feel) ill afterwards, and since then I (not eat) fish at all.
2 Before I (meet) you I (never fall) in love, but now that I (meet) you my life (never be) the same again.
3 Not again! You (always forget) to pay the phone bill! Now they (cut) it off, and it (take) ages to get it reconnected.
4 The tickets (finally come)! The postman (just bring) them. So, we (leave) for Portugal at last!
5 The man over there (smile) at you. I (watch) him for the past five minutes. I think he (decide) to come over here!
6 Before he (die) he (give) all his money to his friends, but when his wife (ask) them to help her, they (say) they (spend) it all.
7 When I (go) in, she (lie) on a sofa. She (hurt) her leg the day before, and she (try) to rest it.
8 I (be) in Madrid this time next week. Some friends of mine (move) there and last week they (phoned) me and (invite) me for a holiday.

5 Put the verbs in brackets in the most suitable forms.

While I (^{1}leave) the pub, I (^{2}see) a familiar face in the car park. It (^{3}be) an old friend of mine, who I (^{4}not see) since we (^{5}be) at school together. It (^{6}not be) long before we both (^{7}sit) inside at the bar, catching up on our news. 'What do you (^{8}do) since we (^{9}leave) school,' I (^{10}ask) Clive, 'you (^{11}seem) to be very prosperous.' He just (^{12}light) a cigar, and at that moment (^{13}drink) a double whisky. 'Well, you never (^{14}believe) this. You (^{15}remember) what I (^{16}be) like at school? At maths especially? I (^{17}get) a job in a local bank, and for a year or two I (^{18}sit) in front of a computer. Then one day I (^{19}have) a brilliant idea; I (^{20}start) using the bank's money to gamble with!' 'You (^{21}joke), of course,' I (^{22}reply), 'or you just (^{23}come) out of jail?' 'Now you (^{24}be) silly,' Clive (^{25}go on). 'I just (^{26}borrow) the money, and (^{27}do) some deals in stocks and shares. All by computer. In fact, I (^{28}grow) richer and richer ever since simply by pressing buttons. Another drink?'

6 Find the errors in each sentence and correct them. (Some sentences are correct!)

1 I am living here ever since I have been 16.
2 When I was a child, I was walking to school every day.
3 I am thinking that I am not liking this very much.
4 Bye! I'm going to see you tomorrow!
5 Oh bother! I leave my umbrella on the bus.
6 By the time I got there they had finished.
7 While he had his breakfast, the postman was knocking on the door.
8 I had visited England many years ago when I was a student.
9 Darling, good news, I will have a baby.
10 Look out! That box will fall on your head!
11 I am swimming every day and I use to go jogging as well.
12 I am not meeting him for two years or more.
13 I see him from time to time.
14 I was always knowing that you have been wrong.
15 I didn't use to like her but I change my mind.

MIXED TENSES

1 Rewrite each sentence, without changing the meaning, beginning as given.

1 He left before I got there.
By the time I _____

2 I haven't seen him since 1987.
The last time _____

3 I was a regular tennis player during my schooldays.
When I _____ regularly

4 In the middle of writing the letter I suddenly remembered something.
While _____

5 There's a dance at our club on Saturday.
We _____

6 I was in Paris for the first time.
I _____

7 You have missed the train by five minutes.
The train _____

8 This block of flats wasn't here before.
There didn't _____

9 They both started giggling during their wedding.
While _____

10 Peter says stupid things, which annoys me.
Peter is _____

11 I'll be here until twelve o'clock.
At twelve o'clock _____

12 A week later, I understood his promise of marriage was a lie.
A week later I realised that when he
_____

13 You are the first person to say that to me.
No-one _____

14 Next year is our fifteenth wedding anniversary.
Next year we will _____

15 A change in the weather is expected.
There _____

2 In the dialogue below, fill each space with a suitable verb in a suitable form.

POLICEMAN: Now sir, when _____ home this morning?

MAN: At about 8 I think. I usually _____ the house at that time.

POLICEMAN: And _____ anything at all? An umbrella, a bag?

MAN: Well, recently _____ at all, so not an umbrella. Just my briefcase.

POLICEMAN: And what exactly _____ you when the two men _____?

MAN: Well, I _____ the road when suddenly one of the two _____ my briefcase.

POLICEMAN: _____ a good look at them by any chance?

MAN: I think I _____ one of them before. He _____ in a garage in Broad Lane.

POLICEMAN: I _____. And _____ of any reason for this attack?

MAN: Well, the money I suppose. There _____ £20,000 in the briefcase.

3 Use the cues below to write the sentences in a letter. Be sure to read all the letter before you begin.

Dear Sir,

1 I/write/about the advertisement which/appear/in last Tuesday's *Evening News*.

2 I/work/as a children's nurse since 1983.

3 Before that I/work as a library assistant but I/not/enjoy the work very much.

4 I/always/love children and I/feel I am the sort of person you/look for.

5 I/visit friends here in Manchester at present and I can attend an interview at any time you/wish.

I look forward to hearing from you,

Yours faithfully,

K. Jones (Miss)

4 Put the verbs in brackets in this text in the most suitable form.

Dear Sue,

I ([1]think) I'd better write and apologise about what ([2]happen) on Thursday. I not usually ([3]behave) that way at parties, but as you probably ([4]realise), I ([5]be) rather drunk when I ([6]arrive). I never ([7]be) as drunk as that before, but I ([8]have) an explanation. You ([9]see), on my way to the party I ([10]meet) this old friend of mine while I ([11]come) out of the pub, which I only ([12]pop) into so as to buy you a bottle of wine. By the time we ([13]talk) over all our news, I ([14]realise) we ([15]drink) rather a lot, but I very much ([16]want) to see you, so I ([17]leave) my car at the pub, and ([18]walk) over. I really not ([19]mean) to break the window, and I ([20]come) round next Monday to repair it myself. I not ([21]think) it ([22]be) very cold in the meantime. I also ([23]write) to your mother and I ([24]apologise) for saying what I ([25]say) to her. You ([26]know) how much I ([27]like) her. I ([28]hope) that by the time I see you next (on Monday) you ([29]forget) my unforgivable behaviour. I ([30]decide) never to drink again.

Your foolish friend,

Ken

5 Match the most suitable endings (a–j) with the beginnings (1–10).

1 This time next week, darling,
2 This is the first time
3 When I left the kitchen
4 The last time I saw her
5 As I'm catching the early plane
6 How often in the past two months
7 Before he became a doctor
8 How long ago exactly
9 When I went there every week
10 Since I started jogging

a did you start having this pain?
b she was trying to learn German.
c I used to feel better.
d we'll be starting our holiday.
e I haven't had a single cold.
f I have ever had a day off.
g the food had started burning.
h I'll be arriving before noon.
i he worked in a travel agency.
j has he turned up late for work?

FIRST AND SECOND CONDITIONALS

1 *What always happens*
If you touch a hot iron, you burn yourself
This could be expressed with *when*:
When you touch a hot iron, you burn yourself.

2 *First Conditional: real condition*
This supposes that there is a real situation, i.e. that you can see what is happening:
If you drop that vase, it will break
In this case, someone is actually holding the vase, so the accident is possible.

3 *First Conditional: real condition + ability or possibility*
The second part of a conditional sentence often includes *can, must,* etc.:
If you break that vase, you can/must bring it to my shop
If you touch this dog, he might bite you

4 *First Conditional: conditional ability*
The *if* clause also often contains *can*:
If you can help me, I'll be really grateful

5 *Second Conditional: hypothetical (unreal) condition (Present/Future)*
This supposes that you can imagine the situation, but it is not real:
If you stole the Mona Lisa, it would be difficult to sell it
You could say this while you were looking at the painting in a gallery, but it supposes that your friend is not really thinking of stealing it!

6 *Second Conditional: hypothetical + ability/possibility; conditional ability*
The same applies as in point 3 above:
If you stole the Mona Lisa, you could hide it
Also as in 4, though this can suggest politeness rather than ability:
If you could help me, I would be really grateful (polite)
If we could turn off the electricity, it would be safer (ability)

7 Contrast of First and Second Conditionals

The important point to remember about the difference between points 1 and 2 above is the difference between what exists in reality, and what you can see only in your mind:

If you jump, you'll hurt yourself (I think you're going to)
If you jumped, you would hurt yourself (I don't think you're going to)

8 Unless

Unless has the meaning of 'only if not':
We'll go there if it doesn't rain = We'll go there unless it rains

EXERCISES

1 Choose which ending is possible for each sentence.

1. I'll give you the money tomorrow
   a if I can.
   b if I could.
2. If you see people running
   a what do you do?
   b what would you do?
3. She wouldn't help anyone
   a if they are in trouble.
   b if they were in trouble.
4. I'll be back here by 6
   a if the train wasn't late.
   b unless the train is late.
5. I would tell you of course
   a if I'll know the answer.
   b if I knew the answer.
6. If no-one calls by next week
   a I would sell the car to you.
   b I will sell the car to you.
7. What will you do
   a if she'll refuse to marry you?
   b if she refuses to marry you?
8. I might possibly lend you my stereo
   a if you promised to be careful.
   b if you will promise to be careful.
9. If there isn't enough for the guests to eat
   a we can phone for pizzas.
   b we would phone for pizzas.
10. If you accepted my advice
    a these things won't happen to you.
    b these things wouldn't happen to you.

2 Put the verbs in brackets in the most suitable form. (Use forms of *can*, *might*, etc. where suitable.)

1. I certainly (leave) on the next bus unless you (make) a decision now.
2. If men from Mars (land) on Earth, people probably (be) scared.
3. If you (not help) me immediately, I (go) somewhere else.
4. I expect that most people (give up) work if they (have) the chance.
5. Generally speaking, if people (eat) too much they (get) fat.
6. What we (do) if it (rain) unexpectedly?
7. I probably (go) to the police if I (lose) my wallet.
8. What you (say) if I (invite) you for a week's holiday in Hawaii?
9. If you (ask) her now, she possibily (accept).
10. If you (be) late, they not (allow) you to enter the room.
11. Unless you (hand over) the money immediately, I (shoot) you!
12. If you (see) her, you (give) her my regards?
13. If you possibly (carry) these bags for me, it (help) me tremendously.
14. If a bomb (go off) here, the result (be) terrible.
15. I (not speak) to him even if he (be) the last person on earth!
16. What we (do), doctor, if he (feel) any pain during the night?

THIRD CONDITIONAL AND CONTRASTS OF FIRST, SECOND AND THIRD CONDITIONALS

1 *Conditional about the past*

a This is a hypothetical condition, since it is impossible to change the past in reality; we can only think about changing it.
If I had tried harder, I would have passed the test
(I didn't try hard enough, and I didn't pass).
The *would have* part is unchangeable; i.e. *I/you/she would have done*, etc.

b It is also possible to have a past action which has an effect on something now:
If he hadn't stolen the money, he wouldn't be in jail
This is a Mixed Conditional; it combines an *if*-clause about the past with a clause about the present, as he is still in jail now.

2 *Conditional + past ability or possibility*
As for the Second Conditional, the Third Conditional can include *could/might*:
If I had tried harder, I might/could have passed the test
(See Units 18, 19 for uses of *could have/ might have*.)

3 *Contrasts of the three main Conditionals and problems*

a The three main conditionals distinguish:
1 Real events = Present + *will*
2 Hypothetical events (now/ Future = Past Simple + *would*
3 Hypothetical events (past) = Past Perfect + *would have*

b *I/you/he/she/it/we/they would* and *would have* are commonly shortened to *I'd/you'd*, etc. and *I'd have/you'd have*, etc.

c *I had* is also shortened to *I'd*, and so it is easy to confuse the meanings of *I'd*. In speech, the /d/ sound of *I'd* may also be lost in the following sound, e.g. *I'd go* may sound like *I go*.

d In the Second Conditional the verb *to be* in formal and written English, is *were* for all persons:
If I were you ... If he were lost ...
In everyday speech, the use of *was* in the 3rd person is common.

e The most common errors in the use of conditional sentences come from confusing the form of the verb, and its meaning. In this example of the Second Conditional, although the form of the Past Simple is used:
if I knew the answer, I would tell you
the verb *knew* does not refer to past time, but to a hypothetical idea.
See Unit 13 for other hypothetical uses of the Past Simple form.

f The difference between the First and Second Conditionals may be a matter of the speaker's attitude. For example, imagine you have just passed your driving test. You say:
If I have an accident, I'll let you know
This suggests that you really expect to have an accident! But:
If I had an accident, I would let you know
means that you can imagine having an accident.

EXERCISES

1 Put the verbs in brackets in the most suitable form. (Use *could*, etc. where appropriate.)

1 If I (notice) that you were waiting I (give) you a lift.
2 I (go) skiing every year, if I (know) how to ski properly.
3 If I (catch) that plane which crashed, I (be) dead now!
4 If we (live) in South America, we (speak) Spanish or Portuguese!
5 I (not lose) the Battle of Waterloo if I (be) Napoleon.
6 I (give up) smoking, if I (be) you; it's bad for you.
7 I (like) you more if you (not laugh) all the time.
8 I (buy) the house before if the price (be) a bit lower.
9 Do you think they (like) this party if they (come)?
10 They (not get) lost last night if they (see) the road-sign.
11 I (phone) you earlier, if I (find) the right change.
12 If you (not leave) your car there, you (not get) this parking ticket.
13 If they (be) friendly, we (not have) all that trouble.
14 If man (not visit) the moon, the world (be) at all different?

2 Complete the missing parts of these sentences. All conditionals are included.

1 If I _____ coming, I would have bought more food.
2 As long as you drive carefully, I _____ my car.
3 I'll talk to you about it tomorrow if you _____ early.
4 If we had left earlier, we _____ the train.
5 If you don't light the fire, we _____ cold.
6 If they _____ how to get here, I would have got lost.
7 Don't give them anything unless they _____ in cash.
8 She would have won the race easily if she _____ faster.
9 You'll feel much better if you _____ an aspirin.
10 If you wrote more letters, your friends _____ reply.
11 If the house _____ in better condition, I would buy it.
12 Let me know at once if you _____ any news.
13 If you hadn't stayed behind, they _____ caught you.
14 You can't take photographs here unless you _____ permission.
15 I wouldn't have done it if he _____ asked me to.

3 Complete each second sentence to comment on the first.

1 We went for a picnic, but it rained and we got wet.
If it _____
2 We can't see very well; you are near the light switch.
If you _____
3 I haven't got enough money to buy a new cassette-player.
If I _____
4 You touched my new dish, and broke it.
If you hadn't _____
5 You always feel tired; it's because you don't take any exercise.
If you _____
6 Your car won't start; I suggest kicking it.
If you _____
7 My advice to you is that you ought to lose weight.
If I _____

WISHES AND OTHER HYPOTHETICALS

1 *Wishes about the present*
This follows the Second Conditional:
If I knew the answer, I would tell you
I wish I knew the answer
Like the Second Conditional, this wish refers to the present.

2 *Wishes about the past (regret)*
This follows the Third Conditional:
If you had told me, it would have been better
I wish you had told me
This kind of feeling about the past is often called a *regret*.
I wish I hadn't eaten so much! (= I feel bad about it now.)

3 *Wishes about ability*
About the present:
I wish I could dance well
About the past:
I wish I could have seen you
Wishes about the future are expressed by the verb *hope*:
I hope you have a good time

4 *Wishes about an annoying habit*
This is very similar to the wish about the present in point 1 above, but is used in annoying situations, when the cause of the annoyance is still there:
I wish you wouldn't smoke in the kitchen!
(I've just found the kitchen full of smoke.)
I wish you didn't smoke in the kitchen (in general)
In speech, the word *wish* is heavily emphasised.

5 *It's time + person*
a This follows the Second Conditional:
If you left, it would be better
It's time you left
b *It's time* has a slightly different meaning from *It's time to*
It's time to take your pill (you always take it at this time)
It's time you took your pill (you have waited too long)

6 *I'd rather* + *person*

   a This also follows the Second Conditional:
      If you told me now, it would be better
      I'd rather you told me now
      It is common as a negative: *I'd rather you*
      didn't smoke
   b Do not confuse this use of *I'd rather* with
      the preference use:
      I'd rather go to the cinema than the
      theatre.

EXERCISES

1 Put the verbs in brackets in the correct form.
(Use *could* where suitable.)

  1 I missed the party. I wish I (be) there.
  2 I'm cold. I wish I (have) a pullover with me.
  3 How many more times! I wish you (listen) more carefully.
  4 This is a lovely place for a holiday. I wish you (be) here.
  5 It's lovely being here. I wish I (not have to) go.
  6 I suppose I like her, but I wish she (not be) so talkative.
  7 Our whole romance was a mistake! I wish I (never meet) you!
  8 I desperately need some scissors. I wish I (find) some.
  9 I wish I (study) harder when I was at school.
 10 Look at this! I wish you (not leave) these dirty socks on the floor.
 11 That water looks lovely! I wish I (learn) how to swim.
 12 You make me wish I (be) ten years younger!
 13 I wish I (not forget) to pay the phone bill.
 14 I wish we (live) in a bigger house in a better district.
 15 I shot him, officer, but now I wish I (not do) it.

2 Complete each second sentence to comment on the first.

  1 We've been here a long time, and it's getting late now.
    It's time _____
  2 I've just missed the last bus home; I haven't got a car.
    I wish _____
  3 I don't want you to tell Sue that I'm buying her a present.
    I'd rather _____
  4 I drank a lot and now I feel ill.
    I wish _____
  5 I don't want him to come now; tomorrow would be better.
    I'd rather _____

  6 My teeth are killing me; I haven't been to the dentist for ages.
    It's time I _____
  7 I left my keys at the office, and now I can't get into the house.
    I wish _____
  8 I don't want you to phone me again please.
    I'd rather _____
  9 We haven't had a talk for ages.
    I think it's time _____
 10 The match is awful; I could be enjoying myself at home.
    I wish _____

3 Complete these sentences so that they make sense.

  1 I really wish _____ and wake me up all the time!
  2 To be honest, I'd rather you _____ and didn't come back.
  3 I think it's high time you _____ and got dressed.
  4 Oh no, it's raining. I wish _____ my umbrella with me.
  5 I wish _____ do that! It's really annoying, you know!
  6 I'd rather _____ . It makes me cough.
  7 It was lovely seeing you. I wish _____ more often.
  8 I'm tired of walking. It's time _____ a rest.

TIME CLAUSES AND TIME WORDS (1)

1 Time clauses
a As in Conditional 1 (see Unit 11), where the *if*-clause uses the form of the Present Simple to refer to future time:
If he comes tomorrow, I'll talk to him
There is the same use of the form of the Present Simple in clauses which begin with the time words which follow:
b *When you arrive, we'll talk about it.*
c *As soon as the film finishes, we'll leave.*
d *I'll wait for you here until you are ready.*
e *After you paint the walls, we'll have a rest.*
f *I'll have lunch before I start work.*
g *By the time we get there, it'll be dark.*
h *Whenever I feel depressed, I'll call you.*
i *Once the dog gets used to you, it won't bark.*
j *The moment you see him, let me know.*

2 Time clauses which emphasise completion
It is also possible to use a Present Perfect tense in a time clause, if the completion of the action is emphasised:
As soon as I have written this letter, I'll do it
And time words can be used in Past time:
As soon as they left, we opened the presents

3 Time words: definite times
(see also Unit 15)
a with prepositions:
   in: *in 1988   in summer, in winter, etc.*
       in March   in the morning,
       in the afternoon, in the evening,
       in the middle of the month
   at: *at 6   at night   at midday,*
       at midnight   at lunch, etc.
       at the end of the week, at the
       beginning of the month
   on: *on Monday, on Monday afternoon*
b *in a week's time* = future reference
   in five years
c *before, afterwards, later*   (See Unit 1)
   I've seen this film before
   I'll see you afterwards (not *after*)
   I'm going to the cinema, I'll see you after that
   I'll see you later
d *ago*
   I left that company two years ago

4 Still, yet, already
a *still* refers to a state which is continuing:
   I still don't know the answer.
b *yet* is normally with *not . . . yet* or in questions, and refers to an event which has not happened:
   They haven't finished yet   I've yet to see her dance
c *already* refers to an event which has happened:
   They have finished already

EXERCISES
1 Put the verbs in brackets in the most suitable tense: Present or Future.

1 When I (come) back from work, I (do) some shopping.
2 Please leave the classroom as soon as the bell (ring).
3 She (stay) in France until she (complete) her studies.
4 I (not phone) them until they (wake) up.
5 Before I (pay) him for the work, I (ask) him to explain the bill.
6 Don't worry, I promise I (go) to the doctor whenever I (feel) ill.
7 After I (finish) cutting the grass, I (water) the flowers.
8 Look, the moment I (finish) the job, I (phone) you.
9 We (not know) the answer until she (tell) us.
10 I (let) you know as soon as I (hear) any news.

2 Put the correct prepositions into each space.

1 We first met _____ a Monday afternoon _____ the beginning of July.
2 I'll see you _____ 8 o'clock _____ two days' time.
3 She was born _____ 15th July, I think _____ 1952.
4 One day _____ April, they met _____ noon and parted _____ the evening.
5 Yesterday _____ breakfast he said he'd see me _____ a couple of days.
6 The roads are dangerous _____ night _____ December.
7 We leave _____ a week's time, I think _____ Tuesday morning.
8 He arrived _____ dinner-time, and left _____ the middle of the meal.
9 I usually get up _____ 7 a.m. _____ summer.
10 The battle took place _____ 25th October 1864.

3 Put a suitable time word or phrase into each space.

1 I didn't understand _____ the time, but _____ I realised what he meant.
2 It's kind of you to offer, but I have _____ done it myself.
3 It wasn't _____ he left that he noticed the window was broken.
4 I'll get there just _____ I possibly can.
5 The baby didn't stop crying _____ night _____ it was six months old.
6 Your order isn't ready _____, but it'll be finished _____ tomorrow.
7 I haven't been there _____, but I know it's sunny _____ July.
8 I have to go home _____ the match, but I'll see you _____.
9 I'm going to that dinner _____ Saturday, but I have no plans for _____.
10 Phone me _____ you arrive, and I'll come if I'm _____ free.
11 It's hard _____ the beginning, but it gets easier _____ you settle in.
12 Don't pay them anything _____ the other bill has been settled.
13 I've _____ got that bunch of flowers you gave me three years _____.
14 He had _____ arrived _____ we got there.
15 Much _____ she explained how she had waited _____ it got dark.

4 Complete each sentence in a suitable way.

1 I'll write to them as soon as _____
2 Don't touch anything in the house until _____
3 There will be a terrible explosion the moment _____
4 I'm sure she will feel grateful whenever _____
5 She won't be really happy until _____
6 I'll put the meat in the oven after _____

TIME WORDS (2)

1 *At first, at last, in the end, at the end,* etc.

a *at first* is in contrast with a change that occurs later:
At first I thought it was raining, but I was wrong

b *at last* suggests relief after a long wait of some kind:
At last it has stopped raining!

c *in the end* is the final result of an action:
I tried three times to pass the test, and I did it in the end

d *at the end* marks the position of something with a beginning and end:
At the end of the film, everyone clapped

2 *Eventually, recently, lately, presently, nowadays*

a *eventually* has the same meaning as *in the end*:
She refused my invitation three times, but eventually she accepted

b *recently* and *lately* have much the same meaning, referring to an inexact time within a period in the past, or to a period of time, but *recently* can also refer to a point of time, while *lately* tends not to have this meaning.
I saw a very good film recently
I have been feeling ill lately/recently

c *presently* usually means *soon* (in GB English); *at present* = now:
I'll be with you presently

d *nowadays* refers to the generalised present, usually in contrast with how things used to be ('in our days' is not possible):
Nowadays more and more people own cars

3 *First(ly)/first of all, secondly,* etc., *finally/lastly/in conclusion*
First of all I would like to thank ...
... and in conclusion I would like to add ...
First we did the shopping ... and finally we paid the phone bill

4 *Periods of time*
a *for, since* and *by*
for a few weeks (refers to the period itself)
since Monday (refers to the beginning of the period)
by Tuesday (refers to the end of the period)

b *from/to*
We stayed there from Monday to Wednesday
to can be replaced with *till*:
The shops are open from 9 till 1

5 Frequency

a *hourly, daily, weekly,* etc. *every day, per week, once a day*:
There are hourly flights to Manchester = every hour.
There are twelve trains a day
They paid her £500 a week/per week

b (See also Unit 5). Less common expressions are:
seldom, hardly ever
frequently, regularly
continuously = without stopping
continually = repeated frequently
They hardly ever ask for my advice
He is continually complaining.

EXERCISES

1 Choose the most suitable time word or phrase in each sentence.

1 I think they are getting married *in/by* 1990.
2 He's been waiting *since/for* weeks to move into that house.
3 I queued for ages and *in the end/at the end* I gave up and left.
4 They paid her £2.50 *per hour/every hour* in the factory.
5 I've *seldom/occasionally* been there, so I can't help you.
6 There are a lot of problems with pollution *presently/nowadays*.
7 Thank you ladies and gentlemen. *First/At first* I'd like to say ...
8 They kept shooting at the target, and *at the end/eventually* hit it.
9 He was expelled from school for *continuously/continually* fighting.
10 There is a *per day/daily* flight to London.
11 They waited for an hour but *at last/at the end* a taxi stopped.
12 I thought he had seen me *at the beginning/at first*, but I was wrong.
13 I saw him *quite recently/quite lately* at the supermarket.
14 They *hardly ever/frequently* go to the pub any more.

2 Put a suitable time word or phrase into each space (see Unit 14).

1 Just _____, I have been thinking a lot about Judith.
2 You should have finished _____ now, I think.
3 We rang the doorbell several times, and _____ we decided she was out.
4 The _____ wage, paid every Friday, is £96.25 before tax.
5 I'm going out now, but I'll see you _____.
6 I had it repaired only last month and it's broken _____.
7 _____, I would like to thank you for listening to me so patiently.
8 Now she has trouble walking, she _____ goes out on her own.
9 I saw her _____, and she seemed a lot better.
10 Stay here _____ it stops raining; you can go shopping _____.
11 _____ you have decided to take some notice of what I've been saying!
12 Sorry to bother you again, but I've never operated this machine _____.
13 The lecture was extremely boring and no-one stayed _____ the end.
14 Just a moment, I'll be finished _____.
15 People tend _____ to work shorter and shorter hours.

3 Find the error in each sentence and correct it (see Unit 14). (Some sentences may be correct.)

1 The shops are open on Saturday at 9 till 1.30.
2 They left at the middle of the film but came back later.
3 I saw her afterwards, and I think she agreed in the end.
4 At last we have had a lot of trouble with the central heating.
5 There were trains at hourly intervals until nowadays.
6 Before you will leave, you must let me show you the garden.
7 Since all the weeks she was in hospital, she felt terribly weak.
8 I couldn't think what to buy him so at the end I got him a tie.
9 He stayed behind in the end of the lesson and talked to the teacher.
10 She's working presently in a solicitor's office.
11 At the time you arrive there, I'll have telephoned the hotel.
12 At first, I would like to introduce you to Mr Sidwell.

FUNCTIONS (1)

Functions are ways of classifying language according to what it is used for. For example, when we make a polite request we can say:

Excuse me, do you think I could borrow your umbrella?

or *Is it OK if I borrow your umbrella?*

What we say exactly will depend on who we are talking to; what we are talking about; how we feel; and so on.

1 Here are three lists of functions, and below them are things people say. Match the names of the functions to the list of language.

1 I'll carry it for you.
2 This is not good enough!
3 If you don't stop, I'll scream.
4 Would you like one of these?
5 The fish is very good today.
6 Sorry, but I'm afraid you can't.
7 Is it all right if I leave now?
8 I'd have the fish if I were you.
9 What do you think I should do?
10 OK, you can have the day off.

a asking for advice
b giving advice
c asking for permission
d refusing permission
e giving permission
f offering something
g offering to do something
h complaining
i threatening
j recommending

b 1 Can you tell me the way to Soho?
2 Hi, how are you!
3 Well, I must go now, so . . .
4 Oh come on, let me try.
5 No, I don't want to.
6 Actually it cost £30.
7 It's much better than yours.
8 Would you like to go for a walk?
9 I wouldn't say that exactly.
10 How about getting her a hat?

a persuading
b correcting
c disagreeing
d making comparisons
e asking for directions
f refusing to do something
g ending a conversation
h greeting someone
i making an invitation
j suggesting

c 1 What do you think about it?
2 Clive, this is Jean.
3 Well, in a way, I suppose . . .
4 Can you close the window?
5 You have to be here at 6.
6 He may have left, I suppose.
7 I'll definitely do it then.
8 You do look nice today.
9 I'm sorry I'm late.
10 Could you tell me what it says?

a making a request
b making a compliment
c asking for information
d introducing someone
e promising
f finding time to think
g apologising
h expressing presence of obligation
i asking for an opinion
j expressing uncertainty

2 Put P next to the most polite/formal ways of speaking.

a Would you mind lending me a pen for just a moment?
b Give me your pen, will you?
c I want to leave early, if possible.
d Do you think I could possibly leave early?
e Sorry I'm late.
f I'm terribly sorry I'm late, but I missed the bus.
g Excuse me, do you think you could tell me the way to the station?
h Where's the station please?

FUNCTIONS (2)

EXERCISES

1 In each pair of sentences, complete the second sentence so that the words perform the function given in the first. Use your general knowledge; not all the language needed is on page 31.

1 Ask permission to leave the room.
  Can I _____ ?
2 Request someone to close the door.
  Do you _____ ?
3 Ask for information about the time.
  Could you _____ ?
4 Apologise for losing someone's book.
  I'm sorry _____ .
5 Invite someone to the cinema.
  Would _____ ?
6 Advise someone to give up smoking.
  If I _____ .
7 Offer to carry someone's bag.
  Shall _____ ?
8 Greet a friend.
  John _____ .
9 Ask for directions to the square.
  Excuse me, could _____ ?
10 Promise to pay someone back next week.
  Look, next week I _____ .
11 Ask for some advice.
  What do you think I _____ ?
12 Give permission for someone to leave early.
  OK, you _____ .
13 Refuse a cigarette.
  No _____ .
14 Offer someone a cup of tea.
  Would _____ ?
15 Suggest that you and a friend go into the living room.
  Why _____ ?

2 Match the reports with the sentences which follow.

1 He advised me not to open the window.
2 She suggested opening the window.
3 She requested me to open the window.
4 He refused to open the window.
5 She offered to open the window.
6 She asked permission to open the window.
7 She promised to open the window.
8 She apologised for opening the window.

a I'm not going to open the window.
b I wouldn't open the window.
c Can I open the window?
d I'm sorry I opened the window.
e Why not open the window?
f Can you open the window?
g Shall I open the window?
h I'll open the window.

Generally speaking, questions are more polite with *Could...*; *Would....*; the added phrase *Do you think...*; and words like *possibly*.

1 *Making and responding to requests*
Do you think you could...?
Would you mind (-ing)...?
Can you...? (less polite)
Do you think you could carry this for me?

'Politeness' may depend on what you ask someone to do; if it seems difficult, or if the person is a stranger, use a polite form. The response is usually either to perform the action requested, and/or say: *Sure, Of course*, etc.

2 *Asking for and giving advice*
What do you think I should do?
What would you do?
I think you should...   I'd... if I were you.

Sometimes a suggestion is given as advice:
Why don't you go on a diet?

3 *Asking for and giving directions*
Excuse me, could you tell me the way to...?
... can you tell me where the station is?
Sure. Go along this road as far as the post office, then turn right
Take the second turning on the left.
It's opposite the bank
Sorry, I'm a stranger here myself. I've no idea, I'm afraid

4 *Asking for, giving and refusing permission*
Can I leave early? (less polite)
Is it all right if I...?   May I...?
Do you mind if I...? Yes, that's all right
Well, I'm afraid...
Well, actually it's a bit difficult

5 *Offering and refusing*
a *an action*
  Shall I do the cooking for you?
  Oh, thanks, that's very kind of you.   Thanks for offering, but...
b *a thing*
  Would you like a cigarette?
  Want a cigarette? (informal)
  Thanks   Yes please
  No thanks, I don't smoke

6 Agreeing and disagreeing
I agree entirely   That's what I think
I agree with Dorothy
I think that's true
I don't quite agree   I can't agree with you
I wouldn't say that
I don't think . . .

7 Inviting and accepting or declining
invitations
Would you like to come to the cinema
tonight?
How about coming for a drink with me?
Perhaps we could go out for a meal next
week?

I'd love to   That would be nice
I'd rather not   I'm afraid I'm very busy
Good idea   I'd love to but . . .

8 Asking for information
Could you tell me what time the next train
leaves?
What time does the next train leave,
please? (more direct)
Do you know what time the next train
leaves, please?

EXERCISES

1 Complete these sentences.

1 Excuse me, do you think
_____ the post office?
2 Excuse me, can you
_____ to the market?
3 Would _____ to lunch
next Sunday?
4 Do you think you _____
radio? It's very loud.
5 I'd _____ but I'm afraid I
_____ that day.
6 Would _____ a drink?
Or something to eat?
7 May _____? I have to go
to the doctor's.
8 If I _____, I
_____ take more
exercise.
9 I _____. In fact, I think
you're completely wrong.
10 Shall _____? I'm going
to the shops anyway.
11 Can _____ here? Or is it
someone else's seat?
12 How about _____
tomorrow? There's a good film on.

13 Could _____? I've just
missed the 9.26.
14 Is it _____ park here? I
won't stay long.
15 Yes, it's quite near. You
_____ this road and
_____ right.

2 Correct anything inappropriate in these mini-
dialogues.

1 Shall you turn on the central heating?
Yes of course, I didn't realise you were cold.

2 Excuse me, is this the right way to the
cathedral?
No, you will go down that street, and you
will turn on the left.

3 Do you have a cup of coffee?
Yes please, that's a good idea.

4 Tell me when the bank opens.
It opens at 9.30, I think.

5 (to a bank manager) The bank will lend me
£30,000, OK?
I'll have to think it over.

6 And in my view, the company needs to
reduce the work-force by 100.
No, stupid!

7 I cut the grass, OK?
Well, it's very kind of you to offer.

8 There will be a party on Saturday. You will
come.
I'd love to, but I'm afraid I'm washing my
hair that evening . . .

3 For each instruction write a question beginning
with the words given.

1 Ask for directions to Harrods.
Do you think _____?
2 Invite someone to dinner.
Would you _____?
3 Offer someone some chocolate.
Would _____?
4 Advise someone not to buy a car.
If _____.
5 Request someone to pass your bag.
Would _____?
6 Refuse an invitation to dinner.
I _____.

CERTAINTY AND UNCERTAINTY—PRESENT TIME

1 *May* and *might*
Both words can be used to express uncertainty, or possibility. There is very little difference between *may* and *might* with this meaning although *might* seems less possible than *may*:
He may still be at home
He might be at home, but I doubt it
Speakers often indicate doubt by emphasising *may* or *might*.
Questions with *may* are not possible, though they are possible with *might*, though rather formal.
Negatives are possible, though must be written in full (= no contractions)
He might not be at home

2 *Could*
Could expresses uncertainty or possibility:
He could still be at home   We could get there by 6
Questions are possible with *could*:
Could he still be at home?
Negatives are possible:
He couldn't be at home

3 *Perhaps* and *possibly*
These words can be used for similar meanings of uncertainty:
Perhaps he is at home
It's possible that he's at home
He's possibly at home

4 *Is bound to; is certain to*, etc.
These phrases express certainty:
He's bound to be at home
He's certain/sure to be at home
They can also be used about future predictions:
United are bound to win the match

5 *Must* and *can't*
These both express certainty and are opposites. *Must not* does not mean the opposite of *must* in this meaning.
He must be at home
He can't be at home
When certainty is expressed with *must/can't*, it does not refer to the definite future. *Is bound to* is used instead.
He is bound to be late on Monday.

EXERCISES

1 Make each sentence uncertain by using the word given in brackets.

1 I think it'll snow tonight.   (may)
2 He is driving there.   (might)
3 They are lost.   (could)
4 She has a cold.   (might)
5 John knows the answer.   (may)
6 They'll get here by then.   (might)
7 She'll lose her job.   (could)
8 I'll tell you tomorrow.   (may)
9 He has one already.   (might)
10 She won't like it.   (might)
11 You'll break it.   (may)
12 They'll lose.   (could)
13 I'll see you later.   (may)
14 I won't be back.   (may)
15 You'll hurt yourself.   (could)

2 Write C (certain) or UC (uncertain) beside the sentences which express these ideas. (Not all the sentences are definitely certain or uncertain.)

1 They're bound to arrive before anyone else.
2 You must pay more attention to your written work.
3 She must be waiting for the bus.
4 You may sit here if you wish.
5 It might be that parcel I've been expecting.
6 He could swim quite well when he was eleven.
7 It could be on that small shelf in the kitchen.
8 She can't be much more than 18.
9 They may not be expecting us if we go now.
10 You may not open your books until I tell you.
11 This old lady might know where they live.
12 They can't lift such a heavy piano on their own.
13 I can see from your books that you must read a great deal.
14 I may not go to the south of France after all.
15 Could I see what it says in your newspaper?

3 Rewrite each sentence without changing the meaning, beginning as given.

1 He can't be here yet.
   I don't think _____.
2 He might not know the answer.
   Perhaps he _____.
3 There's a chance that I'll win the competition.
   I may _____.
4 I'm sure the butler is the murderer.
   The butler _____.
5 Do you think he has it with him?
   Could _____?
6 If you ask him nicely, perhaps he'll agree.
   He _____.

CERTAINTY AND UNCERTAINTY—PAST TIME

1 *May have* and *might have*
These both refer to events in the past which are uncertain:
You may have left it on the bus
He might not have gone by now
The 'have' is unchangeable. As for *may/ might*, use of *might have* suggests that the possibility is slight, although in everyday use, this is shown by intonation. Questions are not possible.
might have can also be used to express annoyance that an action was not performed:
You might have told me there was a policeman behind me!
You didn't tell me, and I am annoyed about this
In speech, *told* would be stressed.

2 *Could have*
This also refers to uncertainty about a past event:
It could have been him I suppose
This way of expressing possibility is close to expressions of ability.
(see Unit 22)
Questions are possible:
Could it have been him?

3 *Is bound to have*, etc.
These expressions show the speaker's certainty about what is likely:
They are bound to have lost it
She is certain/sure to have told him
They suggest that these events are inevitable.

4 *Must have* and *can't have*
These also express certainty, but as a deduction i.e. an opinion of what probably happened:
The butler must have done it
(that's what I think happened)
You can't have seen him yesterday, he's in Australia
(this is my proof that it was impossible)

EXERCISES
1 Rewrite each sentence using the word given in brackets.

  1 I don't think we left the keys at home. (can't)
  2 Perhaps they sold their house. (might)
  3 Perhaps she caught a later train (may)
  4 I suppose it's possible that he took the wrong turning. (could)
  5 I reckon he stole it. (must)
  6 Perhaps she has told him by now. (may)
  7 Knowing him, he probably broke it. (bound to)
  8 It was possible for it to explode. (could)
  9 Why didn't you invite me to your party! (might)
  10 I don't think he was a very good driver, in that case. (couldn't)
  11 I'm fairly sure that they threw it away. (must)
  12 It's possible they had already done it. (may)
  13 You were lucky they didn't kill you! (might)
  14 Perhaps she didn't know about it. (may not)
  15 I think he was drunk. (must)

2 Rewrite each sentence without changing the meaning, beginning with the words given, and using *must, can, might, may, could* where necessary.

  1 He can't have told her the truth.
    I don't think _____.
  2 I'm sure you were a beautiful baby!
    You _____.
  3 I wish you had bought an icecream for me!
    You _____.
  4 She may have taken your umbrella by mistake.
    Perhaps _____.
  5 He won the prize? That's impossible!
    He _____.
  6 Perhaps you dropped your wallet on the stairs.
    You _____.
  7 It's very unlikely that she agreed to that.
    She _____.
  8 Do you think that perhaps he did it?
    Do you think he _____.
  9 I think you have made a mistake.
    You _____.
  10 It's quite possible that he has left by now.
    He _____.
  11 I don't believe that she just grabbed the money and ran out.
    She _____.
  12 That must have been the answer.
    I'm sure _____.

OBLIGATION–PRESENT TIME

1 Must and have to

Generally, the difference between these depends on where the authority comes from:

You have to have a licence to own a gun
                    (an outside authority)
You must lose some weight!
                    (the speaker's authority)

This seems less of a difference with first person:

I must get this letter finished
                    (I'm ordering myself)
I have to get this letter finished
                    (it's a duty)

Here the difference is in the speaker's attitude.

Personal authority is often shown by stressing *must*.

Have to and *have got to* have the same meaning, though have differences in formation (see also Unit 21):

Have we got to go now?   Do we have to go now?
We haven't got to   We don't have to.

The negatives of *must* and *have to* have different meanings:

You don't have to go = It is not necessary.
You mustn't go = You are not allowed to.

have to is often used to form questions and the future tense for *must*:

He'll have to work harder
Do I have to say it again?

2 Should and ought to

These suggest that the obligation is weaker, and may not be kept to:

I really should go on a diet (but I don't have the courage)
You should see a doctor (this is my advice, but you must decide)
He should be here soon (if all goes well)

In formal written language, *should* is often used as a polite expression of obligation:

Members should remove their boots before entering the bar

There is no difference in meaning between *should* and *ought to*. Negatives and questions with *ought to* are formed as *he ought not to/ought he to?*

3 Need and need to

These are formed differently:
I need/Need I/I needn't
I need to/Do I need to?/I don't need to

These can both be used in place of *have to/ have got to* (see Unit 21):
You need a licence to own a gun
You don't need to apply yet

My shoes need cleaning is an idiomatic way of referring to an action which is necessary.

4 Is to/are to

In formal and written language, these are used to express outside obligation, usually as part of a programme:

Students are to arrive by 9 o'clock on Monday 21st July
Candidates are not to bring dictionaries into the examination

This is a much stronger 'order' than the use of *should* in point 2 above.

EXERCISES

1 Choose the most suitable expression in each sentence.

1 I can't understand this form; *must I/do I have to* write my age here?
2 You can't smoke here; it says you *don't have to/mustn't*.
3 After all these lessons, you *have to/should* know the answer!
4 Sorry I can't come, I *should/need* to go to the doctor's.
5 You *don't need to/mustn't* take an umbrella; the sun has come out.
6 If we leave now we *have to/should* be there before 6.
7 This is not good enough! You really *have to/must* be more careful!
8 Any unusual object left unattended *is/has got to be* reported at once.
9 I'm afraid we *must/have to* land at Gatwick Airport because of fog.
10 Danger! You *should/must* not remove the safety cover during operation.
11 Well, I *have to/should* leave, but I'll stay a bit longer.
12 That's all right, you *shouldn't/don't have to be* here till 8.
13 The houses *must/have to* be small because of danger from earthquakes.
14 You *must/have to* tell me all the latest gossip!

2 Rewrite each sentence using the expression given.

1. All members of staff have to report at 7.30. (are)
2. In my opinion, taking a holiday would be good for you. (should)
3. This is serious; it is essential for you to give up smoking. (must)
4. If a table reservation is necessary, let me know. (have to)
5. What's the best thing for me to do if something goes wrong? (should)
6. Do you want me to iron your shirt? (need)
7. Do stay to dinner! (must)
8. If I'm not there on Tuesday, I'll lose the job. (must)
9. You can only play basketball there if you wear proper shoes. (have to)
10. Actually you need a ticket, but I'll let you in. (should)
11. Don't let him get on your nerves too much. (mustn't)
12. A jacket and tie are not necessary. (need)
13. I think you're going to have a good time. (should)

3 Complete each sentence with a suitable use of must, have to, should, etc.

1. The doctor says that she _____ eat salt or it could be fatal.
2. No, it's a very informal party, you _____ wear a suit.
3. I've got a feeling that the oil in the engine _____ changing.
4. You _____ wear gloves or else it could be dangerous.
5. Look, I _____ see you immediately. Meet me at the pub.
6. I suppose I _____ punish you, but I'm not going to.
7. The ship _____ enter the harbour backwards to unload the cars.
8. No-one _____ leave the house without my permission.
9. You _____ admit, it was a really good meal, wasn't it.
10. The worse thing is that I _____ get up at 6 every morning.
11. We _____ hand in that homework on Tuesday or Monday?
12. Jane says she can't come because she _____ visit her granny.
13. Customers _____ park their cars in front of the bank.

OBLIGATION–PAST TIME

1 Must, have to and have got to

had to is used to express the Past tense of must and have to; the negative is didn't have to, question Did you have to? I had to leave early   I didn't have to pay extra

have got to uses the same past form as have to. It is **not** possible to say I hadn't got to pay extra (though this occurs in Reported Speech).

There is another problem with the meaning 'it is forbidden':
They had to pay at once = that was the rule
They didn't have to pay at once = there was no rule
They were not allowed to open the door = the rule said 'no'.

2 Should and ought to

should have done/ought to have done are used to show that an event in the past did not take place, and the speaker feels that a mistake was made:
You should have looked twice before turning left (you didn't)
He ought to have told her before (he didn't)
The have part of the expression is unchangeable.
shouldn't have can also be used to express polite thanks, with a suitable intonation:
That's very kind of you, but you really shouldn't have
This must not be said as if the other person has done something wrong!

3 Need to and need

The past of need to is needed to:
He stayed behind because he needed to finish some work
need is generally only used with negative in the Past as needn't have:
I found that I needn't have gone there
There is a difference of meaning sometimes:
I didn't have to go to school = It was unnecessary, and I didn't go.
I needn't have gone to school = It was unnecessary, but I went.
This meaning of needn't have refers to a mistake (see point 2 above.)
needn't have is also used for polite thanks:
You really needn't have brought so many presents!

4 *Was to*

was/were to and *was/were to have done* refer to an arrangement which did not happen in the end:

She was to have left on Thursday (she didn't in the end)

This has the same meaning as:

She was supposed to leave on Thursday

EXERCISES
(see Units 18, 19, 20)

1 Put each sentence into the Past.

1 Sorry, but I have to leave early.
2 But I'm sure you must know the answer.
3 I think you should tell him the answer.
4 You need to leave me the keys.
5 He's got to come here at once.
6 You shouldn't be so impatient.
7 He must be her new boyfriend.
8 She ought to see him immediately.
9 He must not let the dog into his bedroom!
10 You might try to be a little more friendly!

2 Complete these sentences in the most suitable way (see also Unit 19).

1 When he was in the army he _____ polish his boots.
2 That was stupid! You _____ been more careful.
3 How kind of you! You _____ bought so many flowers.
4 The plane is now an hour late. We think it _____ crashed.
5 My wife isn't with me. She _____ work late tonight.
6 It _____ cost that much; it's only a tiny silver ring.
7 If you're wet, it's your own fault; you _____ worn a raincoat.
8 I missed the last bus and I _____ walk all the way home.
9 Nobody ate a lot; we _____ bought so much food after all.
10 I told you you _____ taken more money with you.
11 I got to the doctor's at 7 and luckily I _____ wait for long.
12 I bought quite a lot of paint but I _____ use it in the end.
13 What _____ do that evening? A lot of work as usual?
14 Instead of turning right, we _____ gone straight on.

3 Rewrite each sentence without changing the meaning, beginning as given using *must*, *have to*, *should*, *need*, etc. (see also Unit 19).

1 Talking to her like that was a mistake.
   You _____
2 He was obliged to leave unexpectedly.
   He _____.
3 Was an operation necessary?
   Did the doctor _____.
4 I'm absolutely sure she told him.
   She _____.
5 How nice, but it wasn't necessary to bring me chocolates.
   How nice, but you
   _____.
6 I'm sure that nothing happened.
   Nothing _____.
7 They told him that making the trip had been unnecessary.
   They told him that he
   _____.
8 Leaving her on her own was a bad mistake.
   You _____.
9 In the end it was necessary for him to spend the night in a hotel.
   In the end he _____.
10 It wasn't necessary for me to think it over.
   I _____.

38

ABILITY AND PERMISSION

1 *Present ability*
can, can't (cannot is more formal):
I can swim= I know how to swim.
I can lift it = I am able to lift the object.

2 *Future ability*
can does have future reference, e.g. *I can come tomorrow.*
With time phrases such as *by this time next week*, which isolate an event in the future, *able to* is used:
He can come next week (we think of the ability as existing now)
He'll be able to come next week (the ability to do so begins next week)

3 *Past ability*
could, couldn't
When I was ten, I could swim
When the actual performance of an act is emphasised, *able to* is used:
He was a good swimmer, and could save people's lives (we don't know whether he actually did save them or not)
He was a good swimmer and could have saved people's lives (he had the ability but didn't use it)
He was a good swimmer, and was able to save people's lives (he actually did it)

4 *Manage to*
This emphasises that a difficulty is involved:
I managed to find the answer in the end, though it was difficult

5 *Permission*
can, could, may (and might) are all used in asking permission:
Can I use your phone?
Could I possibly borrow you lawn-mower? (polite)
May I bring a friend to the lesson tomorrow? (polite)
Might I have a word with you? (very polite)
Other polite phrases include:
Would it be alright if . . .
I was wondering if I could . . .

EXERCISES
(see Units 18, 19, 20, 21)

1 Choose the most suitable expression in each sentence.

1 *May you/Can you* come round for a drink this evening?
2 *Were you able to/Could you* find that book you wanted?
3 What *must/Can* I get you to drink?
4 I phoned three times and in the end I *could/ managed* to get through.
5 *I won't be able to/I couldn't* tell you until I know the answer.
6 I'm sure it *can't/isn't able to* be him; he's on holiday abroad.
7 *May he/Can he* play the piano as well as she does?
8 Luckily she *can/manages* to put us up next week.
9 I tried really hard, but I *couldn't lift/can't have lifted* it.
10 *Could/Should* I possibly leave the dog with you for the afternoon?

2 Rewrite each sentence without changing the meaning, using *can, could*, etc., beginning as given.

1 I'd like your permission to take two days off.
I was wondering if _____.
2 It was impossible for me to buy presents for everyone.
I _____.
3 Meeting tomorrow is impossible I'm afraid.
I'm afraid we _____.
4 I'm sure that isn't the right key; it looks too small.
That _____.
5 Would it be possible for you to help me?
Do you think _____?
6 After a long search she managed to find the right office.
After a long search she _____.
7 They left early so I don't think they enjoyed it very much.
As they left early, they _____.
8 She knows how to speak five languages.
She _____.
9 It's easy to imagine the expression on his face!
I _____!
10 I find it difficult to think of anything to say.
I _____.

3 Put *can*, *must*, *should*, *may*, *might*, etc. in a suitable form in each space.

1 Do you think you _____ turn your record player down?
2 I'm sorry, but you really _____ behave like that in this class.
3 _____ we possibly look at some of those lamps in the window?
4 He _____ helped me, but unfortunately he wasn't there.
5 What about sweets? You _____ certainly cut down on them!
6 I _____ realised that she wasn't going to come to the party.
7 How old were you when you _____ ride a bike?
8 If you ask me, they _____ cheated. That's how they passed.
9 Really! You _____ done the washing up while I was out!
10 What a pity I didn't know. I _____ given you a lift otherwise.
11 You just _____ imagine what Mrs Jones told me yesterday!
12 I suppose I _____ phone her, but I don't feel like it actually.
13 Luckily the docotor was there and _____ help her.
14 The suitcases were really heavy, but I _____ to carry them.

1 *Tenses and Forms*
Examples of tense forms of the verb *to see*:

Present Simple	*I am seen*
Past Simple	*I was seen*
Future	*I will be seen*
Conditional	*I would be seen*
	I would have been seen
Infinitives	*to be seen*
	to have been seen
Gerund	*being seen*
	having been seen
Present Continuous	*I am being seen*
Past Continuous	*I was being seen*
Present Perfect	*I have been seen*

In speech it is easy to confuse *being* and *been*

2 *Agent or no agent*
In a sentence such as:
The money was stolen by one of the clerks
the phrase underlined, the person who performed the action, is known as 'the agent'. It is not always necessary to include the agent in a sentence which has been put into the passive:

Someone has taken my bicycle	*My bicycle has been = taken (the agent is unknown)*
His company dismissed him	*He was dismissed = (unnecessary to include by his company)*

Using the passive is often a way of emphasising the object by putting it first:
Peter broke the vase (subject emphasised; it wasn't Sue who did it.)
The vase was broken (object emphasised; it wasn't the plate.)

3 *Transitive and Intransitive Verbs*
Most verbs can be divided into two classes:
a verbs with a direct object – Transitive:
They ate the oranges
b verbs with no object, or only an indirect object – Intransitive:
Something happened to them
They arrived at the pub

If the verb has a direct object, then it is normally possible to put it into the passive:

The oranges were eaten
However, there are some verbs which cannot be put in the passive; common examples are: *have, fit, suit, look like*
If the verb is intransitive, it may be impossible to make it passive, if the meaning does not allow this, e.g. *happen*.

If the verb has an indirect object, it may be possible to make a passive sentence, especially if the verb describes something done to someone:
They laughed at me   I was laughed at
It would be unusual to say *The pub was arrived at*. The metaphorical use *arrive at a conclusion* can be made passive:
A conclusion was arrived at
See Unit 24 for other related problems.

EXERCISES

1 Find the error in each sentence and correct it so that the verbs are formed correctly.

1 They said that the treasure had being discovered quite recently.
2 They closed the restaurant because the cellar has been flooded.
3 Nothing happened before they were introducing.
4 I have known Sally ever since she and Robert were been engaged.
5 The vase was losing while they were moved house.
6 Everything they were cooked was eaten.
7 When they were reached the airport, the plane was landing.
8 The book was writing by that girl we were met on holiday.
9 It is better to have loving and losing than never loving at all.
10 When I was got to the party, he was been kissed by Judith.
11 The house will be selling as soon as the roof has being repaired.
12 It was lovely to have meeting you.
13 He is been operated on by the doctor some time next week.
14 She is well liking by her colleagues at the library.
15 Good heavens! I was been robbed! Help!

2 Change each sentence into the passive; include an agent if necessary.

1 Some fishermen in a small boat rescued them last week.
2 They have rebuilt the school and made it more comfortable.
3 Someone left this handbag on the seat next to mine.
4 Sophia's boyfriend gave her some gold earrings for her birthday.
5 Last year more than 250,000 people visited this museum.
6 Sue beat Jill in the tennis tournament.
7 They did not invite her to the Christmas party.
8 Everyone remembered that party for a long time.
9 Two men with masks stole the money from the bank.
10 Someone has opened this bottle of orange juice already.
11 They threw it in a corner and forgot about it.
12 We cooked it in the morning and warmed it up later.
13 The police sent him a letter asking him to go to the station.
14 An old man taught her how to play the violin.

3 Change each sentence into the passive where possible.

1 When they returned they found that someone had broken the window.
2 I don't suppose that many people will attend the match.
3 She looked at herself in the mirror.
4 They have knocked down the house we lived in then.
5 That shirt they gave you really suits you.
6 She has found the ring she lost last week.
7 When the accident happened, everyone ran down the stairs.
8 The car crashed into a tree but no-one was injured.
9 The last time I saw her she looked much better.
10 They told each other the answers to the questions.
11 I had a party last week but very few people came.
12 The police arrested a man and charged him with murder.
13 The beer I drank that night seemed very strong.
14 They built their house where an old tower had once stood.

PASSIVE (2)

1 Get/have something done
a for things which we make happen –
   often services done for us by someone
   else:
   They had their house repainted
   (someone else did it)
   I'll have you arrested (I'll make it happen)
b for things which happen to us – often
   accidents or misfortunes:
   She had her car stolen
   He had his arm broken
c When *get* is used, it can suggest that *we
   managed to do something*:
   We got the wall painted in the end (it
   was difficult but we did it)
   We got the wall painted (we paid
   someone to do it)

2 Reports
In news reporting especially, when a report
involves opinion (*people say . . .*) it is
common to use an impersonal expression:
It is said . . .
This can also involve putting the object of
the report (*people say that he*) at the
beginning of the sentence:
*People say that he is in prison = He is said to
be in prison*
Verbs which are commonly used in this way
include:
*believe, say, report, know, understand,
suppose, think, admit*
Here are examples of the forms of the
infinitive involved:
He is believed to live in Brazil
= People believe he lives in Brazil
He is reported to be travelling to Brazil
= People report he is travelling to Brazil.
He is thought to have left Brazil
= People think he left/has left Brazil.
*He is understood to have been asking for
help*
= People understand he was asking for
help.

3 Verbs with two objects
Some verbs (e.g. *give*) can have two objects:
We gave her the watch
It is possible to make two different passive
sentences:
She was given the watch
The watch was given to her

Other verbs like this (with *to*) include:
*lend, offer, bring, owe, promise, show,
throw*

4 Other problems with Passive
a *make* (= force) requires *to* when passive:
   *He made them stop = They were made to
   stop*
b passive sentences may include the
   instrument rather than the agent:
   The door was opened with a screwdriver
c with *there*:
   A new shop has been opened
   There has been a new shop opened

EXERCISES
(see Unit 23)

1 Rewrite each sentence without changing the
meaning, beginning as shown.

1 The dentist took out all my front teeth.
  I had _____
2 The car was lent to him by an old friend.
  He _____
3 The hijacker made them lie face down on
  the floor.
  They _____
4 Everyone knows he is a terrible liar.
  He _____
5 She managed to do the ironing in the end.
  She got _____
6 He was thought to have sold secrets to a
  foreign power.
  Everyone thought _____
7 He was thrown a rope by someone on the
  bridge.
  A rope _____
8 Someone broke his arm in a fight.
  He _____
9 There is a report that he is seriously ill.
  He _____
10 They have just removed her appendix.
  She _____
11 A glass of water will be brought to you if
  you call.
  You _____
12 Everyone supposes that she is coming on
  Saturday.
  She _____

2 Rewrite each sentence without changing the meaning, beginning as shown.

1 When the accident happened, he was taken to hospital.
   They _____

2 He was made to rewrite the report.
   They _____

3 I wasn't asked for my opinion of the matter.
   Nobody _____

4 Our whole building was redesigned by an architect from London.
   We _____

5 They say that the president was shot by the secret service.
   The president _____

6 They used a knife to open the french windows.
   The french windows
   _____

7 An old man with a walking-stick showed me the way
   I _____

8 You shouldn't have taken those boxes away.
   Those boxes _____

9 Nobody thought she was really dangerous.
   She _____

10 You can't make people do things they don't want to do.
   People _____

11 Everyone thinks she is the best person for the job.
   She _____

REPORTED SPEECH (1)

1 *Backshift or not?*

a Generally, when a reporting verb in the Past tense begins a report, then all following tenses are *backshifted*, i.e. they go back into the past:
'I've lost my job,' he said = He said (that) he had lost his job
'I know the answer,' she said = She said (that) she knew the answer
'I'll call her,' he said = He said (that) he would call her
If the reporting verb is in the present, there is no backshift.

b Backshift may be omitted when the report stays true for the present:
'It's on the corner of Byron Road,' she said
She said it's on the corner of Byron Road
Some speakers would prefer to use backshift here, however.

c In colloquial speech, a reported series of events in the past is not usually shifted into Past Perfect:
'I was getting near the corner, when suddenly a dog ran out in front of the car and I skidded into a tree.'
She said that she was getting near the corner when a dog ran out in front of the car and she skidded into a tree

2 *Questions, commands and exclamations*

a indirect questions are not asking for answers and do not follow the usual formation of questions. They are either *wh-* questions:
She asked me what my name was
He asked me where I was staying
or Yes/No questions:
She asked me if/whether I wanted a drink

b commands usually involve using *tell* or *order*:
Put it on the shelf = She told me to put it on the shelf
They may also involve paraphrase, i.e. not all the words are reported:
For heaven's sake, get lost! = She told me to go away

c exclamations are difficult to report word for word, and paraphrase is usually involved:
What a fantastic new coat = He admired her new coat.

3 Reference words

All references to people, places, times, etc. change in indirect speech because the point of view has changed, or the meaning of the reference is no longer the same:

'I'm visiting my granny' = She said she was visiting her granny
'I'll see you here' = He said he'd see me there
'Give me that book' = He asked me to give him the book
'Meet me next week' = She asked me to meet her the following week

Times whose meaning depends on a reference in the present generally have an indirect version:
today becomes *that day*
tomorrow becomes *the next/following day*

Paraphrase is sometimes necessary:
'It's over there!' = He told me where it was

EXERCISES

1 Report each sentence, beginning *'She said . . .'*

1 I don't want to stay here until tomorrow.
2 I haven't found that book I lost yesterday.
3 I won't be here when you come back.
4 I'll see you the next time you're here.
5 He's the last person I want to meet.
6 I have no idea what time I'll be back.
7 When he came back I still hadn't finished.
8 You're the second person who has told me that.
9 This is the last time I'll tell you.
10 I'll be arriving on Saturday evening.
11 I haven't changed my mind about it yet.
12 No-one knows the answer as far as I am aware.
13 I'm leaving early in the morning.
14 This is the horse I bought yesterday from Alan.
15 Nothing I ever do seems to turn out right.

2 Report each sentence beginning, *'She asked me . . .'* or *'She told me . . .'*

1 Do you know when the next train leaves for Canterbury?
2 Don't put too much paint on the brush.
3 Have you ever been to Naples in January?
4 When does Terry get back from the hairdresser's?
5 You are a stupid idiot.
6 What are you going to do when she finds out?
7 Leave that wet umbrella by the door please.

8 Don't work too hard! You'll wear yourself out.
9 Why haven't you replied to the letter I sent you last week?
10 Am I supposed to be coming round to your house tonight?
11 Do you have to go to the dentist tomorrow morning?
12 Take the rubbish downstairs when you go.
13 Is there anything good on television tonight?
14 Who was the girl I saw you with yesterday?
15 What's on at the cinema at the end of this week?

3 Which words were actually spoken?

1 He told me to drop the gun or else he would shoot.
2 She asked me whether I wanted her to sign the form.
3 He said he would be dropping in on his way home that evening.
4 They asked whether they could talk to the director.
5 He said he would meet me at the airport the following day.
6 She asked me what the small red button was for.
7 He told me to leave the office and not to come back.
8 She asked me why I had been following her.
9 She told me to put down the parcels, and showed me where.
10 He asked me what exactly I wanted him to tell me.
11 They said they had been waiting since early that morning.
12 She told me it was a stupid thing to do.
13 He asked me whether I had dropped the paint on his shoes.
14 She told me she never wanted to see me again.

REPORTED SPEECH (2)

1 *Paraphrase (see Unit 25)*
Although we often report every word someone has said, it is often impossible to do this.
'Oh really, don't be so silly.' = *She told her not to be so silly*
As well as this, we tend naturally to summarise and generalise what we have heard; it is not only impossible to remember every word, but it would be very annoying if someone reported irrelevant information:
He said that he liked the place could be a report of:
Well, I suppose it's rather a good place/Gosh, isn't this a nice place.

2 *Reporting words*
a *say, tell*
He said it was going to rain
He told me it was going to rain.
b *offer, refuse, accept*
She offered me a drink   She offered to lend me her books
I asked him to work late but he refused
He refused to work late (he didn't want to)
They accepted my invitation
c *deny*
He denied stealing the money/He denied that he had stolen the money (it was not true)
d *greet, interrupt*
These both describe actions, and do not report words:
She greeted them   He interrupted me
Note: *greet* can only be used for what is said when you meet someone, not when you say goodbye.
e *reply, complain, admit*
He replied that he thought she was wrong   He replied to her
She complained that the water was cold   She complained to him
She complained about the water
He admitted that he was wrong
He admitted doing it
f *agree, promise, advise, decide*
She agreed that it was a good idea
She agreed with him
She agreed to do it
He promised to help her   He promised he would help

They advised me to wait   They advised me that I should wait
We decided not to go   We decided against going
g *suggest, apologise, insist*
I suggested taking a bus   I suggested we should take a bus   I suggested that we took a bus
He apologised for being late
I insisted on helping them
h *explain, confess* (= more serious than admit)
She explained that she had missed the bus   She explained it to me
He confessed that he had taken the money   He confessed to the crime

EXERCISES

1 Match the reports (1–15) with the reporting words (a–0), and then report each sentence (if this is possible).

1 Hello, nice day isn't it?
2 I lost my keys, you see.
3 They make a lot of noise.
4 Would you like a sweet?
5 I'm sorry I forgot your birthday.
6 I'll definitely do it tomorrow.
7 Oh thanks, I would like a drink.
8 Right, I'm going to tell them.
9 I'm not going to leave this room.
10 Yes, I did break the vase.
11 You really must try some pie.
12 I'm not a member of that club.
13 If I were you I'd change jobs.
14 Yes, I think you're right.
15 Shall I carry it for you?

a She accepted _____
b He apologised _____
c She admitted _____
d He decided _____
e She denied _____
f He advised _____
g She offered _____
h He offered _____
i She complained _____
j He explained _____
k She refused _____
l He insisted _____
m She greeted _____
n He promised _____
o She agreed _____

COMPARISON

2 Rewrite each sentence without changing the meaning, beginning as given.

1 He apologised to her for breaking her camera.
I'm sorry _____

2 I can assure you, Mr Smith, that this will not happen again.
She promised _____

3 Would you like one of these oranges, John?
He offered _____

4 He complained about the socks they always left in the bathroom.
'You are _____!'

5 It's not true! I didn't steal the money!
He denied _____

6 Look, why don't we go for a little drive in the country?
He suggested _____

7 He advised her to leave the dog in the garden all day.
'If _____'

8 She decided to buy the green one with long sleeves.
'I'll _____'

9 You see, what happened was that the car broke down.
He explained _____

10 Don't leave those books on that shelf in the sun, Mary.
He told _____

3 Put a suitable reporting word into each space.

1 She _____ it was the last time she would be working there.

2 He _____ on my having another drink, and I couldn't refuse.

3 She _____ me very rudely I was an idiot.

4 He _____ that he had murdered the old man for his money.

5 They _____ for not phoning before they came round.

6 He _____ to bring the radio back as soon as possible.

7 She _____ them tea, but they said they had just had some.

8 They were _____ to take at least £300 with them on the trip.

1 *Comparing with adjectives*

a *I think this book is **longer than** that one.*
*I thought that film was **more interesting than** the other one.*

b *It is **not as entertaining as** the other one.*
*I don't think it is **as entertaining as** the other one.*
*It doesn't seem **as interesting as** the one we saw last week.*

c *The book about archaeology is **the longest** (of them all).*
*The French one was **the most interesting** (of the three we saw).*
*The seats in the front are **the least expensive**.*

d *I thought they were both **just as interesting**.*
*The French one was **as interesting as** the Italian one.*

2 *Problems with the formation of adjectives*

a *good   better   (the) best*
bad   worse   (the) worst
far   further   (the) furthest
(farther, farthest)
old   elder   (the) eldest (for describing ages of people)

b When to use *more/most*
Adjectives of one syllable:
normally add *-er/-est*
long = longer/longest
Adjectives of two syllables: those ending as below add *-er/-est*
-er e.g. *clever*
-y e.g. *happy*
-ow e.g. *yellow*
-le e.g. *gentle*
Note: these are adjectives with underline final syllables.

Other two-syllable adjectives:
normally use *more/most*
That mountain seems more distant
Adjectives of more than two syllables: use *more/most*
It's more unreliable

3 Comparing with adverbs

a adverbs generally add *more/most*:
   She finished the work more quickly than her brother did

b some adverbs which are the same as adjectives add *-er/-est*:
   late, hard, fast, slow, early

c irregular forms:
much	*more*	*most*
well	*better*	*best*
little	*less*	*least*
badly	*worse*	*worst*

4 Spelling problems

a one-syllable words which end in a single consonant with a single vowel before it double the consonant:
   fat = fatter   cool = cooler

b words ending in a consonant and *y*, change *y* to *i*:
   happy = happier

c words ending in *e* add only *-r, -st*:
   rude = ruder

EXERCISES

1 Complete each sentence with a suitable word or words.

1 My brother is so slow; I can run _____ he can.
2 There is no difference in weight; this one is _____ that one.
3 In my company the boss is lazy and doesn't work _____ we do.
4 All six were expensive, but the gold one was _____ the others.
5 This beach is the cleanest because it is _____ from the city.
6 She drove carefully but very _____ and we arrived in no time at all.
7 I can't understand this; it's _____ book I've ever read.
8 I didn't like the meal; I don't think it was _____ the one before.
9 Yes, the meal was bad; one of _____ I've ever eaten I think.
10 I left one of the jobs till last because it was _____ important.
11 Dick is a famous writer, but Clive is _____ well known.
12 Both of these are good, but the third is easily _____.
13 Which do you think is _____, cold weather or wet weather?
14 My sister isn't _____ in the family; I have a brother of 40.
15 I play football _____ I used to, because of my bad knee.

2 Rewrite each sentence without changing the meaning, beginning as given.

1 Dorothy is a much better swimmer than Alan.
   Alan can't _____
2 This chair is more comfortable than those other two.
   Those two chairs aren't _____
3 This is the least tasty of the cakes we've tried.
   The other cakes we've tried were _____
4 The other students in that class aren't as clever as Wendy.
   In that class, Wendy is _____
5 No-one in my office works as hard as Ken.
   Ken is the _____
6 I've never seen a garden as peculiar as this one before.
   This garden is the _____
7 Peter knows more about boats than anyone else here.
   No one here knows as _____
8 We should use my plan; it's easier than yours.
   We should use my plan; it's not _____
9 All the other washing-machines are more expensive than this one.
   Of all the washing-machines, this one is _____
10 The organisation of the conference was not very good.
   The conference was not very _____

3 Find the errors in each sentence and correct them. (Some sentences may be correct.)

1 It's a better solution as the one you suggested yesterday.
2 She is easily the more intelligent in her family.
3 He is really not as lazy than he seems.
4 This is the worst spaghetti I have ever tasted.
5 She is much better paid than her sister is.
6 The uncomfortablest chair has got the more cushions in it.
7 It's less expensive but much difficult to use.
8 She is as better as she was the last time we saw her.

RELATIVE PRONOUNS

1 *Which* and *who*

a *which* refers to things:
He bought a house. It cost a lot of money = He bought a house which cost a lot of money
Note: *it* is not repeated.

b *which* can also refer to a subject clause:
She lost her purse, which annoyed her very much
It is *not possible* to leave out this *which*

c *who* refers to people:
He bought the house from a woman. She lived in West Africa = He bought the house from a woman who lived in West Africa
Note: *she* is not repeated.

d in both the examples above, it is also possible to use *that*:
He bought a house that cost a lot of money
He bought the house from a woman that lived in West Africa
This is common in everyday speech.

2 *Whose*

whose means 'of who':
I met a friend. Her husband works with my husband = I met a friend whose husband works with my husband
Note: *her* is not repeated.

3 *What* = the thing(s)

What I want to know is, where are they?
Nobody knows what he told her

4 Defining and non-defining relative clauses

a Defining clauses give us important information about the subject:
The girls who were late had to wait outside
This tells us *which girls* are being described, suggesting that there are other girls who did not have to wait.
It is possible in everyday speech to use *that* instead of *who*.

b Non-defining clauses give extra information about the subject:
The girls, who were late, had to wait outside

The important information here is:
The girls had to wait outside
and the extra information *who were late* has a comma on each side.
It is not possible to use *that* in this kind of clause.

5 *Whom*

a *whom* is the object form of *who*, and is mainly used in more formal language:
I met a friend whom I had not seen for years

b In everyday language it is more usual to use *who*:
I met a friend who I hadn't seen for years

c *whom* is necessary after a preposition:
The friend from whom I borrowed the book wants it back
In everyday speech it is more usual to say:
The friend I borrowed the book from wants it back (see point 6 below).

6 Leaving out *who* and *which*

a If the phrase before *who, which (that)* is the subject of the clause, it is *not possible* to leave out *who, which (that)*:
That girl who is looking at you is my cousin

b If the phrase before *who, which (that)* is the object, then *who, which (that)* can be left out.
The girl I met yesterday has now left
The purse I lost last week has been found

EXERCISES

1 Tick each sentence in which *who(m)* or *which*, can be left out. (In some cases this is possible if the word order is changed.)

1 He had to stop several times, which annoyed him a lot.
2 That is the assistant who sold me the faulty clock.
3 The man who I spoke to yesterday told me something different.
4 The last person, who was an old lady, got on the bus.
5 He asked me who I wanted to talk to.
6 I don't know the name of the shop from which I bought it.
7 He picked up the letter which I had just written.
8 I'd like you to tell me who I'm speaking to.

9 He was someone who I used to know a long time ago.
10 The last person who spoke to me was the manager.

2 Put *who(m)*, *which*, *what*, *whose* or nothing in each space as necessary.

1 He didn't know _____ had paid him, _____ was strange.
2 Someone _____ had been there before told us the way.
3 _____ I ought to do, is find out _____ gloves they are.
4 Peter, _____ car had broken down, met a man _____ managed to fix it.
5 The drawer in _____ he found the gun was the one _____ I had searched.
6 Those _____ come late must stay to do the work _____ they have missed.
7 The dog _____ I bought was the one _____ you saw the day your arrived.
8 That is the boy _____ mother knows the man _____ repaired our fridge.
9 He is the one _____ asked me _____ I gave the money to.
10 The snow, _____ had been falling all day, was _____ gave us trouble.

3 Join each group of sentences using the words given in brackets and beginning as shown. Make any other necessary changes.

1 A man brought the letter. He left it on the table. (who)
The man _____
2 I have a friend. Her six children sing in a choir. (whose)
I have _____
3 I sold my car to a man. You spoke to him. (−)
The man _____
4 The cup was on the table. It had tea in it. (which)
The cup _____
5 I bought a painting. I sold it to a friend. He liked it. (who)
I sold the _____
6 A student came late. I borrowed her pen. (whose, who, the one)
The student _____
7 I went on holiday. I went with a friend. He has fallen ill. (whom)
The friend _____

UNIT 29

INFINITIVE

1 *Verbs followed by the full infinitive (with **to**)*

1 I earn very little and so I *can't afford to* buy a car.
2 My neighbour *agreed to* look after my cat while I was away.
3 We *aim to* reach the top of the mountain by 6 this evening.
4 I *arranged to* meet her outside the cinema at 8.30.
5 She *was determined to* pass the exam at the first attempt.
6 He *was prepared to* do anything to keep his old job.
7 Please *don't bother to* see me out, I know the way.
8 We *chose to* take the slow train, which was a mistake.
9 I *decided to* buy her a pair of gloves for her birthday.
10 I *demand to* see the manager at once.
11 You *deserve to* succeed because you have worked so hard.
12 I *expect to* arrive there at about 4.
13 The train *failed to* arrive on time yet again.
14 I *hope to* see you all again next year.
15 She *learned to* drive while she was at school.
16 I *long to* lie on the beach in the sun and relax!
17 She finally *managed to* find her purse after searching for ages.
18 They *offered to* give me a lift, but I turned them down.
19 She was *pretending not to* notice that I was there.
20 I *promise to* return your book as soon as possible.
21 The doorman *refused to* let me go in.
22 It *seems to* be raining, I'm afraid.
23 English people *tend to* drink a lot of tea.
24 He *threatened to* punch me in the face!
25 Do you *want to* dance?
26 I *wish to* make a complaint.
27 I *would like to* live on the other side of town.

2 *Verbs with objects and full infinitive:*
 1 I *asked him to* show me the way.
 2 We *expected them to* arrive earlier.
 3 The robbers *forced her to* hand over the money.
 4 He *invited me to* visit his house in the country.
 5 I *reminded her to* lock the door.
 6 My uncle *is teaching me to* ride a horse.
 7 They *told me not to* be so silly.
 8 He *warned them not to* step on the broken stairs.

3 *Verbs followed by the bare infinitive (without to)*
 1 My parents *let me stay out* as late as I like.
 2 They *made me clean up* the mess I had made.
   BUT I *was made to* clean up the mess I had made. (passive)
 3 *I'd rather go* to the cinema than stay at home.
 4 I think *you'd better go* to the dentist's.
 5 *can, could, shall, will, would, should, must, might, may* are followed by the bare infinitive.

EXERCISES

1 Put a suitable verb from page 49 in each space, in an appropriate form.

 1 I thought it was wrong so I _____ to do it.
 2 I really can't _____ to go abroad for my holidays this year.
 3 Although the boxes were very heavy, we _____ to carry them.
 4 Disc jockeys on the radio _____ to speak in an annoying way.
 5 I _____ to be a foreigner, and the policeman let me drive on.
 6 I'm so tired! I'm simply _____ to get to bed and sleep.
 7 We _____ to meet here at 6, but there is no sign of the others.
 8 The teacher _____ to punish them if they made too much noise.
 9 It started raining, so we _____ to go to the pub for a drink.
 10 Everyone thought that she _____ to win the prize.
 11 I'll try my best, but I can't _____ to get back by 7.
 12 While I was wondering what to do, a woman _____ to help me.

 13 It took me six months to _____ to walk again after the accident.
 14 That road _____ to lead towards the mountains; shall we try it?
 15 They _____ to pay the money on time, and so couldn't sit the exam.

2 Rewrite each sentence without changing the meaning, beginning as given.

 1 He said that he didn't want to sit at the front.
   He refused _____
 2 She succeeded in getting through to the office in the end.
   In the end she managed
   _____
 3 His parents wouldn't allow him to buy a powerful motorbike.
   His parents wouldn't let
   _____
 4 Going on a package tour was your choice.
   You chose _____
 5 I had to stay late at the office last night.
   My boss made _____
 6 'Leave the dog alone, Jean,' said Chris.
   Chris told Jean _____
 7 I really ought to phone the doctor.
   I'd better _____
 8 You're supposed to take one tablet every two hours.
   You should _____
 9 Taking a holiday in August is common in Britain.
   The British tend _____
 10 Actually I'd prefer to go dancing with Margaret.
   Actually I'd rather _____
 11 'Turn off the lights, won't you,' she reminded them.
   She reminded them _____
 12 They made her write the test a second time.
   She was made _____
 13 You needn't do the washing up, I'll do it.
   Don't bother _____
 14 'Would you like to come to my party, Christine?' said Ron.
   Ron invited _____
 15 I'm really looking forward to seeing Judith again.
   I really long _____

INFINITIVE AND -ING FORMS (1)

The -ing form of verbs is used after the italicised verbs in these sentences.

1 You should **avoid** *lifting* heavy weights for a while.
2 It's not **worth** *waiting* any longer, she's not coming.
3 The old man **denied** *stealing* the tin of tomatoes.
4 I really **dislike** *working* on Saturday.
5 I **enjoyed** *meeting* them very much.
6 I **fancy** *going* out for a meal tonight. How about you?
7 When we **finish** *eating* we'll go for a walk.
8 I can't **help** *falling* in love with you.
9 Can you **imagine** *living* in a huge house like that?
10 He **keeps** *phoning* me in the middle of the night.
11 I don't **mind** *helping* you, I've nothing else to do.
12 Would you **mind** *moving* your car please? It's in the way.
13 I really **miss** *living* in London now I have moved.
14 He **practises** *making* his speeches in front of a mirror.
15 They **prevented** her (from) *escaping* by locking the door.
16 I can't **recollect** *meeting* him before.
17 Don't **risk** *leaving* the cases in the car, they'll be stolen.
18 I can't **stand** *getting* up early in the winter.
19 I **suggest** *taking* the bus as far as the village, and then *walking*.

See Unit 32 for verbs followed by to or -ing with change of meaning.

EXERCISES
(see also Unit 29)

1 Put the verb in brackets into the most suitable form: infinitive with *to*, bare infinitive, or -ing form.

1 I'm afraid that I can't stand (sit) on chairs like that one.
2 I went back to the office and demanded (speak) to the director.
3 She didn't really fancy (go) to the cinema, so she stayed at home.
4 I hope (meet) a lot of interesting people while I'm there.

5 She always pretends not (hear) what people say to her.
6 I used to enjoy (listen) to pop music, but my tastes have changed.
7 I don't think we should risk (arrive) too late at the airport.
8 They warned Ronnie (be) more careful about what he said to people.
9 Terry keeps (ask) me to lend her my notes from last week's lesson.
10 I wish you'd let me (help) you with that ironing.
11 The doctor told me to avoid (walk) up stairs for a week.
12 I don't think she deserves (lose) her licence for such an offence.
13 If you've finished (read) the paper, could I have a look at it?
14 They decided that they should practise (speak) as much as possible.
15 She promised (let) me know the results as soon as they came out.

2 Put the verb in brackets into the most suitable form, as in Exercise 1 above.

1 When did you learn (knit) so well?
2 In the winter months I miss (lie) in the sun on the beach.
3 Although I put out my hand, the bus failed (stop).
4 It's time you decided (leave) home and get a flat of your own.
5 I can't really imagine Brian (ride) a camel, can you?
6 In the end he chose (travel) by bus rather than by train.
7 Excuse me, but would you mind (open) the door for me?
8 Everyone here is longing (see) you when you come at Christmas.
9 I think I would like (lie) down for a bit, if that's alright.
10 Do you mind (wait) for the steak a few minutes longer?
11 The main idea is to prevent the other team (score) more goals.
12 No, funnily enough I don't recollect ever (meet) you before.
13 This part of the country tends (have) a lot of rain in spring.
14 Could you arrange for someone (collect) the parcel for me?

3 Put the verb in brackets into the most suitable form, as in Exercise 1 above.

1 I think they'd rather (watch) the film on the other channel.
2 They are threatening (cut off) the phone unless we pay the bill.
3 The sun is shining now, but I think we'd better (take) raincoats.
4 Well, I suggest (ask) everyone to bring a bottle of something.
5 When I speak to her, she doesn't seem (understand) what I say.
6 He didn't bother (set) the clock, so they overslept.
7 She keeps (leave) her umbrella on the bus.
8 I don't think I am prepared (lend) you any more money.
9 She tried to make me (change) my mind, but I didn't.
10 Have you managed (fix) the radio yet?
11 He said that he fancied (take) a trip to the coast tomorrow.
12 The soldiers were made (clean up) all the mess they had made.

INFINITIVE AND -ING FORMS (2)

1 *Verbs followed by* **to** *or* **-ing**
These verbs can be followed by *to* or *-ing* with little change of meaning. The difference is small: *to* is used for particular situations, *-ing* for general ones. It is not normally a mistake to use one form only.

a I **can't bear going** to bed late.
  I **can't bear to** see him at the moment.
b I **hate waiting for** buses in the rain.
  I **hate to tell** you, but your house is on fire!
c I **like/love swimming** as long as the water is warm
  I **like/love to swim** on Sunday mornings
d I **prefer walking** to driving
  When I go to work I **prefer to walk**
  I **would prefer to walk now**
e I **propose leaving** this point until the next meeting (= a suggestion)
  I **propose to sell** this house next year (= a plan)
f It has **started snowing/to snow**

2 *Changes of meaning which depend on* **to** *or* **-ing**
a I **meant to tell you** (= an intention)
  This **means telling** everyone as soon as possible (= involves)
b I **regret doing** that   (= I'm sorry I did it)
  I **regret to tell** you that   (= I'm sorry I have to)
c I **remember locking** the door   (= it's in my memory now)
  I don't **remember locking** the door.   (= it's not in my memory)
  I **remembered to lock** the door   (= an event of remembering)
  I **forgot to lock** the door.   (= an event of forgetting)
d I **stopped to drink** some water   (= I stopped because I was thirsty)
  I **stopped drinking** water   (= I didn't continue)
e I **tried to take** the aspirin   (= it was difficult)
  I **tried taking** an aspirin   (= to see if it would help)

3 *Verbs of perception*

Verbs of perception (particularly *see*, *watch*, *hear*) have change of meaning depending on bare infinitive or *-ing*.

a *I **saw him eat** the cake* (the action was complete; *he ate it*)

*I **saw him eating** the cake* (incomplete; *he was eating it*)

b *I **watched them leave** the room* (complete)

*I **watched them leaving** the room* (incomplete)

c *I **heard her sing** the song* (complete)

*I **heard her singing** the song* (incomplete)

EXERCISES

(see also Units 29 and 30)

1 Put the verb in brackets into the correct form: infinitive + *to*, bare infinitive, or *-ing* form.

1 I hope he'll remember (post) my letter. It's very important.
2 Do you really enjoy (work) until ten in the evening?
3 They stopped (eat) because they were so hungry.
4 We didn't like the idea of writing a test, so we refused (do) it.
5 When you were at school, were you made (play) football on Saturdays?
6 I tried (pick) the apples, but the branch was too high to reach.
7 I saw him (put) the chocolate in his mouth, and (swallow) it.
8 I'd like (get up) early on Sundays, but it's difficult.
9 I must admit that I regret (leave) the job I had in Leicester.
10 You wouldn't mind (help) me push the car, would you?
11 She said that she meant (tell) you, but she forgot.
12 I don't think you'd better (leave) until the rain stops.
13 If you prefer (wait), you can sit here in my office.
14 What exactly do you remember (do) when you got there?
15 Have you tried (drink) lemon and honey? That's good for colds.

2 Put a suitable verb into each space.

1 She _____ taking the tablets as soon as she felt better.
2 You won't _____ to buy me some cigarettes, will you?
3 I think I'll _____ talking to her, when she leaves.
4 I really can't _____ being rich and famous!
5 Do you _____ not going to university when you had the chance?
6 Their teacher _____ them to bring their workbooks.
7 I heard him _____ the letter and then leave.
8 Would you _____ to stay at a hotel, or in a bed and breakfast?
9 I _____ having to stand in a queue. It drives me mad!
10 If you are a serious dancer, it _____ practising every day.
11 I arranged to meet her here, but she _____ to turn up.
12 I _____ to tell you that you have not been accepted for the job.

3 Put the verb in brackets into the correct form: infinitive + *to*, bare infinitive, or *-ing* form.

1 I think the boss should make some of us (work) a lot harder.
2 Why did they decide (move) from such a lovely house?
3 If the washing-machine doesn't work, try (give) it a good kick!
4 If you stopped (worry) so much, you would feel much better.
5 Hadn't you better (make) an appointment with the doctor?
6 How could anyone forget (turn off) the cooker and (go) out?
7 If you really enjoy (dance), then we could enter the competition.
8 She didn't stop (eat) all day; no wonder she is overweight.
9 You really must (try) not to make so many mistakes.
10 They seem determined (succeed) however long it takes.
11 If you'd rather (take) a taxi, I can phone for one.
12 You say your job is difficult, but you should try (do) mine!
13 If I take that job, it will mean (leave) home much earlier.

PHRASAL VERBS (1)

The term 'phrasal verb' covers four main kinds of verbs combined with prepositions or adverbials. Units 32, 33, 34, 35 give practice in these four types. In some exercises you will need a dictionary. Notice that some phrasal verbs have more than one meaning.

1 *Verbs with three parts*

In these verbs, the third part is a preposition, so the object must follow; the object cannot be put between the parts. An adverb can be put between the second and third parts of some of these verbs.
*She gets on with her neighbours **very well***
*She gets on **very well** with her neighbours*

2 *Examples*

a *I'm trying to **cut down on** smoking, from ten a day to five a day.*
*We must try to **cut down on** what we spend; we're short of money.*

b *You go now, and **I'll catch up with** you later.*
*She missed school for a month, and couldn't **catch up with** the others.*

c *I don't think I **feel up to** going out; I feel very tired.*
*I'd like to go to the party, but I don't **feel up to** it. I've got flu.*

d *He was cheating in the exam but he **got away with it**. He wasn't caught.*
*If you kill me, you'll never **get away with it**. The police will know.*

e *Don't look at the ceiling! **Get on with** your work!*
*I must **get on with** my homework, it's already eight o'clock.*

f *I'm afraid I don't **get on with** my boss. We just don't agree.*
*Do you **get on with** your wife's parents? Do you all like each other?*

g *You're going too fast! I can't **keep up with** you.*
*She likes to **keep up with** all the latest fashions.*

h *Her neighbours **look down on** her because she wears old clothes.*
*They **looked down on** him because he came from a poor family.*

i *I **look forward to** receiving your reply to my letter.*
*I'm really **looking forward to** my next holiday.*

j *Your behaviour is unacceptable! I will not **put up with** it!*
*He **puts up with** so many problems and never complains.*

k *The car has stopped. We've **run out of** petrol!*
*Could you go to the shops for me? I've **run out of** sugar.*

l *Don't just run away. You must learn to **stand up for** yourself.*
*We must all **stand up for** what we think is right.*

EXERCISES

1 Look through the examples of three-part phrasal verbs. Complete the sentences below, using an appropriate verb in the right form.

1 Oh bother! I've _____ _____ _____ ink. Can I use your ballpoint?
2 Stealing his car is a crazy idea. You'll never _____ _____ _____ it.
3 I must have a rest. You walk on, and I'll _____ _____ _____ you.
4 I feel that everyone _____ _____ _____ me because I'm badly dressed.
5 I'm really _____ _____ _____ meeting my penfriend for the first time.
6 He's so rude to you! Why do you _____ _____ _____ him?
7 I've got lots of work to _____ _____ _____, so I must go now.
8 Rest for a week, and then you'll _____ _____ _____ working again.
9 When we go jogging, I can never _____ _____ _____ her.
10 Don't let him tell you what to do; _____ _____ _____ yourself.
11 You have to be able to _____ _____ _____ people in this job.
12 We must _____ _____ _____ the amount of time we spend phoning.

PHRASAL VERBS (2)

2 Match the most suitable endings (a–j) with the beginnings (1–10).

1 He's a difficult person. He doesn't get
2 You're silly. Why do you put
3 You must work faster if you want to keep
4 He's so lucky. He always gets
5 I don't believe in looking
6 If you want to save money, try cutting
7 What a great idea! I'm looking
8 Don't come if you don't feel
9 I can't always help you. You must stand
10 We can use jam if we run

a up for yourself.
b down on sweets.
c forward to seeing them.
d out of honey.
e on with many people.
f away with everything.
g up with his rude remarks?
h up with the rest of us.
i down on the poor.
j up to meeting them all.

3 Rewrite each sentence without changing the meaning, beginning as shown, and using one of the verbs from examples on page 54.

1 We haven't got any toothpaste left.
We have _____
2 He parks his car there and is never caught.
He always _____
3 I really like the idea of going dancing tomorrow.
I'm _____
4 I'm not really well enough to travel so far by bus.
I'm _____
5 If you don't fall behind with the work, you'll pass the exam.
If you _____
6 She has a very good relationship with her parents.
She _____
7 How does he stand the way she treats him.
How _____
8 We'll have to use less coal this winter.
We'll _____
9 Please continue doing what you have got to do.
Please _____
10 Lots of people think they are better than gypsies.
Lots of people _____

1 a A second type of phrasal verbs has two parts which can be split by putting the object between the verb and the particle; or the object can go after the particle:
He **filled in** the form
He **filled** the form **in**

b It is not possible to put *me, him, her, it, them* at the end of these verbs.
Jim **knocked** him **out**   I **picked** it **up**
Put them **back**

c If the object is described in a lot of words, then it is better to put it after the particle:
Jim **knocked out** the big man with the scar on his cheek

2 *Examples*
(Check meanings with a dictionary as well.)

1 *My aunt **brought** me **up**, as my parents lived abroad.*
2 *They **called off** the match half an hour before the start.*
3 *Can you **clear up** your room; it's so untidy.*
4 *If you make a mistake, **cross** it **out**.*
5 *Please **fill in** the form with all your personal details.*
6 *He **gave away** all his money to the poor before he died.*
7 *I've been trying to **give up** smoking, but I can't stop.*
8 *When you finish the test, **hand** your papers **in** to the teacher.*
9 *The robbers **held up** the bank and took half a million pounds.*
10 *As he crossed the road, a bus **knocked** him **over**.*
11 *The robber hit me on the head with a vase and **knocked** me **out**.*
12 *Question 6 was hard so I **left** it **out**.*
13 *I didn't know what it meant so I **looked** it **up** in the dictionary.*
14 *Please lend me £10 and I'll **pay** you **back** on Friday.*
15 *I'll **pick** you **up** at 7, so be ready when I ring your doorbell.*
16 *I'm **putting** some money **aside** each week for my holiday.*
17 *The match was **put off** from Saturday to the following Monday.*
18 *If you need somewhere to stay, we can **put** you **up** for a night or two.*

19 *I **rang** her **up** this morning but she didn't answer the phone.*

20 *A group of American businessmen **took over** the company.*

21 *I've decided to **take up** skiing this winter.*

22 *When I **tried** the coat **on**, it was the right size, but I disliked it.*

23 *Let's **try out** the new engine and see if it works.*

24 *He asked her to marry him, but she **turned** him **down**.*

25 *Turn the radio **up**; I can't hear it with all that noise outside.*

26 *Turn the light **off** will you?*

27 *I **wore** myself **out** playing tennis and had to rest.*

28 *I've looked at the problem twice, but I can't **work out** the answer.*

29 *Every night before I go to sleep I **wind up** my watch.*

30 *Tell me the address and I'll **write** it **down**.*

EXERCISES

1 Replace part of each sentence with one of the verbs in the list of examples on pages 55 & 56, in the correct tense.

1 If you don't know the answer, search for it in the encyclopedia.

2 I offered him £50,000 for the house but he rejected the offer.

3 Can you put your personal details on this form, please?

4 Some Italian friends of mine gave me a bed for a week.

5 She decided to save some money every month for her retirement.

6 If you give him the details he'll calculate how much tax you'll pay.

7 I've decided to start collecting stamps as a hobby.

8 Three armed men robbed the National Bank yesterday.

9 I'm afraid Jack is ill, so can we postpone the meeting until Tuesday?

10 As he left the room he extinguished the light.

11 She decided to stop eating chocolates.

12 She phoned him to invite him to her party.

13 Can you come and collect me in the car?

14 My company has decided to buy the shares of Jones Ltd.

15 Can you make your room tidy before you go to bed, please?

2 Fill in the spaces in the sentences with verbs from the list on pages 55 & 56, in a suitable form.

1 Please _____ your books _____ at the end of the lesson.

2 _____ _____ children is not an easy job in my opinion.

3 As we talked, the journalist _____ everything _____ in her notebook.

4 When I _____ the shoes _____, I realised they were too small.

5 One boxer hit the other so hard that he _____ him _____.

6 Don't worry, I'll _____ you _____ all the money by next month.

7 They _____ the meeting _____ only an hour before it was due to begin.

8 I wrote the wrong address on the form, so I _____ it _____.

9 They _____ themselves _____ by working so hard and not relaxing.

10 An old lady was _____ _____ by a car right outside our house.

11 Don't forget to _____ _____ the alarm clock before you go to sleep.

12 We had so many apples this year that we _____ some _____ to friends.

13 I can't hear the music very well; can you _____ it _____?

3 Match the most suitable endings (a–j) with the beginnings (1–10).

1 Last week the manager left
2 It's hard for me to work
3 It's a good idea to give
4 It's very kind of you to put
5 Sorry, but I've got to put
6 It's really difficult to give
7 I think we should try it
8 When I tried it
9 She got up and turned
10 When I suggested it he turned
11 I wish you wouldn't turn
12 Last night she rang

a on it was obviously too big.
b the radio up so loud.
c the party off until next week.
d out before we decide to do it.
e out the answer in my head.
f me up and asked for some advice.
g the idea down immediately.
h him out of the team again.
i us up for so long.
j up things you really like.
k off the lamp by the door.
l away things you don't need.

PHRASAL VERBS (3)

There is a group of two-part verbs which do not have an object:
Their car broke down and so they had to take it to a garage

Examples

1 *When the washing machine **broke down**, we called the repair service.*
2 *After she fainted, it was nearly a minute before she **came round**.*
3 *This flower only **comes out** if you keep it in a warm place.*
4 *Why don't you **call in** when you're on your way home?*
5 *As I opened the front door, I saw a taxi **draw up**.*
6 *He started the course, but **dropped out** before the end of the term.*
7 *They used to be good friends, but they **fell out**.*
8 *We tried to arrange a holiday with them, but the plan **fell through**.*
9 *The prisoner climbed over the wall and **got away**.*
10 *She kept asking her parents for permission, until they **gave in**.*
11 *I found the problem too difficult, so I **gave up**.*
12 *That meat you forgot to put in the fridge has **gone off**.*
13 *Sorry to keep you waiting; can you **hang on** a bit longer?*
14 *I was talking to her on the phone, but she suddenly **hung up**.*
15 ***Look out!** That pile of books is going to fall on your head!*
16 *She began to feel faint, and then she just **passed out**.*
17 *They sent him four letters before he finally **paid up**.*
18 *They had driven a long way, so decided to **pull in** and take a rest.*
19 *It rained all morning, and they decided it had **set in** for the day.*
20 *We packed our bags, locked the doors, and **set off**.*
21 *I can't stand the way that boy is always **showing off**.*
22 *The plane went down the runway and **took off**.*
23 *It hurt but the pain is **wearing off** now.*
24 *He suddenly **turned up** yesterday after a year abroad.*

EXERCISES

1 Rewrite each sentence using a verb in a suitable form from the list on this page.

1 The shoplifter was chased by a policeman but managed to escape.
2 I knew you lived near my office so I decided to make a visit.
3 The flight to London left the airport at 6.15.
4 Some people faint when they see blood.
5 We saw apples for sale by the road, so we stopped and bought some.
6 We haven't been seeing one another since we stopped being friends.
7 The car stopped working in the middle of the desert.
8 After calling her four times without success, I stopped trying.
9 She was trying to impress us by telling us about her big house.
10 He regained consciousness after the operation feeling much better.
11 They told me to be careful, because the stairs were broken.
12 I asked him for the money he owed me and he gave it to me.
13 Guess who came to the party last night?
14 By the time I got home with the fish, it had started to smell bad.
15 When I asked her to come out with me, she put down the phone.

2 Fill the gaps in each sentence using a verb from the list on this page in a suitable form.

1 I feel much happier when the flowers start to _____ _____ in spring.
2 I'm not sure if Mr Jones is in. Can you _____ _____ for a moment?
3 This pill may make you feel sleepy, but that will soon _____ _____.
4 We _____ _____ early because we wanted to miss the heavy traffic.
5 A Rolls Royce _____ _____ outside her house, and an old man got out.
6 When he goes to a party, he always _____ _____ in front of the girls.
7 You may think I'm going to change my mind, but I won't _____.
8 It looks as if the bad weather has _____ _____ for the weekend.
9 She was in the team for today, but she _____ _____ at the last moment.
10 She left home after she _____ _____ with her parents.

PHRASAL VERBS (4)

11 When the plane _____ _____,
I thought it was going to crash.

12 The road is very dangerous at the moment,
so _____ _____ .

13 I know this is difficult, but don't
_____ _____ ! Keep trying!

14 We had to wait for ages because the train
had _____ _____ .

15 They agreed to buy the company, but the
plan _____ _____ in the end.

3 Choose a word or phrase (a–j) which could
replace the underlined words.

a escaped   e leave   h blossomed
b be careful f fainted   i woke up
c arrived   g stopped   j stopped
d quarrelled   trying

1 When the bus drew up outside the museum,
nobody wanted to get off.

2 Look out! You're going to drop the plates.

3 They fell out because he was more
interested in watching football.

4 If we set off now, we'll be there before it
gets dark.

5 When all the flowers came out, the garden
looked beautiful.

6 People who turned up without tickets were
not allowed in.

7 I tried to catch the butterfly with my hands,
but it got away.

8 Nobody answered me when I knocked on
the door, so I gave up and left.

9 The room was so hot that several people at
the back passed out.

10 Suddenly everything went black. When I
came round, I was alone.

Verbs in this group have an object, but
cannot be split:
*I'm looking for Alan. Do you know where
he is?*

Examples

1 *Your watch will be ready in a few days.
You can **call for** it on Friday.*

2 *While I was painting the cellar, I **came
across** this old vase.*

3 *Of course I'll help you. You can **count on**
me.*

4 *Oh dear, there isn't any sugar. We'll
have to **do without**.*

5 *She was very ill for a while, but she has
got over it now.*

6 *They **went over** the papers carefully
looking for mistakes.*

7 *She didn't have much money so had to
live on less than £5 a week.*

8 *The nurses **looked after** me very well
when I was in hospital.*

9 *I've been **looking for** that pen for ages.
Where did you find it?*

10 *The police are **looking into** last week's
robbery at the school.*

11 *We spent most of the morning **looking
round** the old part of the city.*

12 *I'm **making for** London, but I don't
know exactly where I'm going.*

13 *I **ran into** John the other day at the
cinema quite by chance.*

14 *I'm going to the garage to **see about**
ordering a new car.*

15 *Don't worry about posting the letters,
I'll **see to** it.*

16 *The manager **sent for** him and asked
him for an explanation.*

17 *I'm **sitting for** the examination next
year if all goes well.*

18 *Our teacher won't **stand for** any
whispering during tests.*

19 *The letters BBC **stand for** British
Broadcasting Corporation.*

20 *She **takes after** her mother; they both
have the same good looks.*

21 *She kissed the frog and it **turned into** a
prince.*

EXERCISES

1 Fill in the spaces with suitable verbs from the list of examples on the previous page.

1 When I was a student, I had to _____ _____ money my parents gave me.
2 It started as a friendly argument but _____ _____ a fight.
3 If you're interested in buying the house, come and _____ _____ today.
4 We've _____ _____ the doctor, but he may take a long time to get here.
5 The escaped prisoner is thought to be _____ _____ Birmingham.
6 If you are too busy to make lunch, I can _____ _____ it.
7 The abbreviation etc. _____ _____ et cetera.
8 The landlord said he would _____ _____ the rent every Friday.
9 The other day I _____ _____ my old boss at a party.
10 You're being unfair, and I'm not going to _____ _____ it.
11 You can always _____ _____ him to say something silly!
12 The manager promised to _____ _____ her complaint.
13 Before you leave, we should _____ _____ the plan just once more.
14 I must go, as I have to _____ _____ finding a new baby-sitter.
15 If we go out tonight, who is going to _____ _____ the baby?

2 Match the most suitable endings (a–j) with the beginnings (1–10).

1 He says he's making for
2 Everyone says I take after
3 We'll just have to do without
4 She is still looking for
5 He will never get over
6 She is going to sit for
7 I think we should look into
8 Tomorrow I'm going to call for
9 I wouldn't stand for
10 He wanted to look round
11 Yesterday I came across
12 We should see about
13 I don't want to run into
14 I think we should go over
15 No-one can live on

a the shirt I left at the shop.
b some interesting old photos.
c the university exams next week.
d getting passports quite soon.
e what we have written once more.
f anyone who knows who I am.
g so little money.
h a few little luxuries.
i that gold bracelet she lost.
j the nearest garage.
k my Uncle Jim, but I disagree.
l the death of his little dog.
m the circumstances of her death.
n such bad behaviour as that.
o the whole building.

3 Replace the italicised words with verbs in a suitable form from the list of examples on page 58.

1 I have decided to *investigate* this matter personally.
2 It will take you a week or two to *recover* completely from 'flu.
3 Most people seem to think that he *resembles* his father.
4 You can't *rely on* her always to arrive on time, I'm afraid.
5 I've got to *arrange about* the flowers we need for the garden.
6 Guess who I *met* yesterday? My old friend Noel from the bookshop.
7 We'd better *check* the figures again before we send the letter.
8 How do you *put up with* his silly behaviour?
9 I'll *collect* the photographs at the end of the week.
10 She *took* the exam when she was only 13 and passed.
11 I *discovered* an interesting book in the second-hand shop yesterday.
12 I can't *manage without* chocolate at least once a day!
13 I *took care of* their cat when they went abroad on holiday.
14 She's been *trying to find* a new flat for weeks without success.

ADVERBS OF DEGREE

1 *So* and *such*

a *So* + adjective:
It was so cold that I had to wear two pullovers

b *Such* + (article) + adjective + noun:
It was such a cold day, that I stayed at home
They were such old chairs, that no-one wanted to buy them.

c there is also the formal *so* + adjective + article + noun:
It was so cold a day, that I stayed at home

2 *Too* and *very*

a *too* can mean *also*; it is placed at the end of the sentence.
I like sweets, and cakes too
This can only have a positive meaning. In negative meanings, use *not ... either* or *neither ... nor*
I don't like sweets, and I don't like cakes either
I like neither sweets nor cakes

b *too* has a similar meaning to *very*. The difference is that *too* includes the meaning of ability.
It's very cold today. We can't go swimming
It's too cold today to go swimming
This soup is too hot to eat (Note: *to be eaten* is not correct)
(This soup is too hot for me to eat)

c *(not)* + adjective + *enough*:
Is the soup hot enough?
It's not warm enough to go swimming today

3 *Rather* and *quite*

a *rather* can be used with either positive or negative adjectives:
You are being rather silly   (a little)
It's rather good isn't it?   (unexpectedly)

b *quite* is usually used with positive adjectives:
It was quite good   (not as much as I expected)

c *quite* can also mean *completely*:
He isn't quite ready yet

EXERCISES

1 Rewrite each sentence without changing the meaning, beginning as shown.

1 The room was so dark that I couldn't read.
The room was too _____

2 He is so tall that his head touches the ceiling.
He is such _____

3 You are too young to see this film.
You are not _____

4 I feel very tired and don't want to work.
I feel too _____

5 That wall is too high to climb.
That wall is so _____

6 This bag is too heavy to carry.
This is such _____

7 This food is so hot I can't eat it.
This food is too _____

8 These trousers are too old for me to wear.
These are such _____

9 They couldn't play tennis because the weather was very bad.
The weather was too _____

10 I didn't get there in time to catch the post.
I wasn't early _____

11 It was raining so hard that I stayed at home.
There was _____

12 The film was too long to enjoy.
The film was so _____

13 I waited for so long, that I became impatient.
I waited for such _____

14 I don't think you are experienced enough for the job.
I think you are too _____

15 These cakes are so stale we can't eat them.
These cakes aren't _____

2 Put *too, very, enough, quite, rather, so,* or *such* in each space.

1 Sorry, but I haven't _____ finished yet.

2 She used _____ long words that we didn't understand.

3 I decided to go out because I felt _____ miserable.

4 I'm afraid this crossword is _____ difficult for me.

5 I thought the film was _____ interesting, but nothing special.

6 It's not really dry _____ to use yet.

7 These rooms are just _____ large to keep warm properly.

8 That's _____ kind of you, but I'm afraid I can't.

9 Is your bed comfortable _____ ?
10 I feel _____ disappointed that I could cry!
11 It was a tight fit, but the car was just large _____ to hold us all.
12 Thank you very much, that was _____ tasty.
13 I ate some _____ , but I didn't like it.
14 He was _____ fat to wear such tight trousers.
15 The snow wasn't good _____ for skiing.

UNIT 37

VERBS AND PREPOSITIONS

1 To
a see Units 3 and 4 for uses of *to* with places, and verbs of motion.
b see Units 29, 30, 31 for uses of *to* which are part of the infinitive.
c the following commonly used verbs use *to* as a preposition, so *to* is followed by a noun or the *-ing* form (gerund) of the verb.
admit (to)   be used/accustomed to
confess to   listen to something
look forward to   object to
prefer something to something

2 Of
accuse someone of
approve/disapprove of
die of something
rob someone of something   warn of

3 With
agree with someone   deal with
provide someone with   share something with   trust someone with something

4 For
apply for   care for   vote for   wait for

5 On
blame something on someone
concentrate on   congratulate on
depend on   insist on   rely on someone

6 In
believe in   confide in   involve someone in
specialise in   succeed in   take part in

7 About
boast about   know about
make up (your) mind about   talk about

EXERCISES
1 Put a suitable preposition into each space:
1 I'm afraid I don't agree _____ you about the meeting.
2 Quite a lot of people I know believe _____ the supernatural.
3 The secretary eventually confessed _____ stealing the money.
4 I've been waiting ages _____ the chance to talk to you.
5 She says she is looking forward _____ meeting us at Easter.

6 They accused the journalist _____ blackmailing the politician.
7 Nobody warned them _____ the dangers involved in the experiment.
8 I'm sorry, but I must insist _____ seeing the manager at once.
9 He died _____ tuberculosis at the early age of 32.
10 She was there at the time but didn't take part _____ the discussion.
11 There's nothing I like better than listening _____ good music.
12 She saw the job advertised and applied _____ it at once.
13 The trouble is that there is no-one I can confide _____ .
14 In my job I have to deal _____ people most of the time.
15 To be honest, I'm not used _____ getting us as early as this.

2 Put a suitable preposition into each space.

1 I wish you would make up your mind _____ what you want.
2 No one would admit _____ taking the book from my desk.
3 While she was ill her neighbours cared _____ her.
4 She doesn't approve _____ my staying out so late.
5 He's always boasting _____ his rich relatives.
6 I don't object _____ your smoking, as long as you open the window.
7 She trusted her friend _____ all her secrets.
8 On the way there, he was involved _____ an accident.
9 I prefer swimming _____ playing tennis.
10 When things go wrong, they always blame everything _____ me.
11 I'm sharing a flat _____ two girls from Leeds.
12 She told them that she knew nothing _____ it.
13 I must congratulate you _____ passing the exam. Well done!
14 I wouldn't trust him _____ my money!

3 Put a suitable verb or phrase from page 61 into each space, in the correct form.

1 After several attempts, they finally _____ in opening the trunk.
2 When you start work here, we'll _____ you with a uniform.
3 He spends all his time _____ about football, I'm afraid.
4 A place at university will _____ on your examination results.
5 Our company _____ in helping overseas clients.
6 He keeps promising to do things, but you just can't _____ on him.
7 On the way to the hotel, they were _____ of all their money.
8 You must stop going out so much, and start _____ on your studies.
9 I decided to _____ for him at the last election.
10 You don't really _____ in Father Christmas, do you?
11 I'm _____ to going away on holiday, because I need a rest.
12 She was _____ of copying her answers from someone else.
13 Don't worry, I'll _____ with the problem. You can go home.
14 He was unhappy at work and decided to _____ for a new job.
15 My mother doesn't _____ of my having a punk haircut.

PREPOSITIONS (3)

1 Prepositions following adjectives

at good/bad at surprised at
in interested in
of fond of full of guilty of
    jealous of
on keen on

2 Prepositional phrases

a get on/off (a bus, train, plane;)
   get in/out (a car, a window;)

b at

at lunch	at home
at once	at first
at times	at the moment
at sea	at war
at least	at work
at 100 kph	at present
at school	at peace
at the same time	at last
at the beginning/	
end	

c by

by bus etc.	by post	by oneself
by chance	by mistake	by sight
by heart	by name	by accident
(take) by surprise		
ten metres by five metres		

d for

A is for apple	a cheque for £20
for sale	for a change
it's good/bad for you	for example

e in

in bed	in prison	in town
in love	in trouble	in private/public
in half	in pieces	in two
in fact	in any case	in particular
in a way	in debt	in danger

f on

on business	on holiday
on board	on a diet
on duty	on fire
on the left/right	
on a journey/trip/voyage	

g out of

out of date	out of reach
out of stock	out of work
out of order	out of control
out of practice	out of (petrol)

h up

up to date	it's up to you

EXERCISES

1 Put the most suitable preposition in each space.

1 I'm not very good _____ history; I'm more interested _____ physics.
2 When I got _____ the horse after my ride, I wished I'd gone _____ foot.
3 He explained that he wasn't really fond _____ children.
4 She is jealous _____ me because I don't have to go _____ a diet.
5 Everyone _____ board the ship felt seasick _____ first.
6 When I went to Greece, I was surprised _____ how cold it was.
7 I tried to get _____ the bus, but it was full _____ people.
8 He was found guilty _____ murder, though he killed her _____ accident.
9 She sat in the kitchen _____ herself, learning the poem _____ heart.
10 While we were _____ holiday, we realised we were _____ love.
11 Their house is _____ sale because they are _____ debt.
12 That country is _____ war, and you can't send things there _____ post.
13 I was _____ school _____ the same time that you were.
14 _____ private he admits that it all happened _____ mistake.
15 Before the policeman went _____ duty, he went shopping _____ town.

2 Put the most suitable word or phrase in each space.

1 We bought the chair _____ , and glued it together ourselves.
2 Mr Jones is away _____ the moment. Can I help you?
3 When the fire brigade arrived, the fire was _____ .
4 I was walking to work when I met her completely _____ .
5 The car must have been doing _____ 200 kilometres an hour.
6 _____ I feel very tired, but not very often I suppose.
7 The books we use have not changed for years and are very _____ .
8 I know her _____ , but I don't actually know her name.
9 He broke the bar of chocolate _____ , and they each had a piece.
10 I suppose you are right _____ , but I don't really agree.

11 I'm sorry, madam, but we are _____.
Can we order it for you?
12 Her sudden arrival took me completely
_____.
13 The police told him that he was
_____, and should not go out.
14 We export food products, _____ olive
oil.
15 Never mind that we can't get tickets. I didn't
want to go _____.

3 Complete each sentence with one suitable
word.

1 The apples at the top of the tree were out of
_____.
2 When the warning was given, they left the
building at _____.
3 I have a small flat of my own in
_____.
4 After the first lesson, the teacher could call
everyone by _____.
5 They had to abandon the ship because it
was on _____.
6 Sorry, you can't use this ticket. It's out of
_____.
7 I picked up someone else's umbrella by
_____.
8 When he was a boy, he was always in
_____ with the police.
9 We had a fantastic time on _____,
and want to go back next year.
10 I saw him next morning at _____,
drinking his coffee alone.
11 At _____ the film seemed dull, but in
the end I enjoyed it.
12 The lift is out of _____, so you'll have
to use the stairs.
13 We waited for ages, and at _____ a
taxi came by.
14 I'm not doing anything in _____
tonight, so I can come.

(see also Unit 55)

1 *All, each, every* and *both*
a *all* is not usually used alone; *everything* is
used instead.
All (of) my books have disappeared
They took all my things.
Everything has disappeared
They took everything.
b *each* refers to two or more separate
things:
*They each have a dictionary and a
notebook* (*every* is not possible here)
*Each person in the office has a
cup* (*every* is possible here)
c *every* is used for a collection of things:
*Every person in the room was
crying* (emphasises the total)
*Each person in the room was
crying* (emphasises individuals)
d *every* always takes a singular verb.
Each can have a plural subject, and so
may have a plural verb.
e *both* refers to two things and takes a
plural verb:
both of them were late *Both John and I
have colds*
f *both* can be used with *and*:
*She was both easy to talk to and
interesting to know*

2 *Neither, none, not . . . either*
a *neither* refers to two things and takes a
singular verb:
Neither of them has a bike
I don't know, and neither/nor does he.
b *none* means 'not any of'. It refers to a
larger group.
None of them knows the answer.
c *neither . . . nor* negates two things:
*He neither cleaned the wall nor washed
the floor.*
(He didn't clean the wall, he didn't wash
the floor.)
d *not . . . either* can be used to give the
same meaning:
*He didn't clean the wall, and he didn't
wash the floor either.*

3 Much, many, little, few
(see Unit 55)

a *many* is used for countable things in question form, and with *not*:
Have you got many flowers in your garden?
I haven't got many trees.

b It is very formal to use *many* in statements:
I have many trees.
It is more usual to use *a lot of/lots of.*

c *much* is used for uncountable things in question form and with *not*:
Have we got much money left?
We haven't got much time

d It is not possible to use *much* in statements.

e *few* is used for countables; it is not used in questions or with *not*:
I have few bottles left

f *a few* has a more positive meaning:
I have a few friends (not many, but luckily some!)
I have few friends (not many, and I'm unhappy)
a few is often made stronger and partly negative with *only*:
I have only a few friends (some, but not really enough)

g *little* is used in the same way as *few*, but for uncountables:
I have little money left (negative)
I have a little money (positive)
I have only a little money (some, but not enough)

EXERCISES

1 Rewrite each sentence without changing the meaning, beginning as shown.

1 There is no food left.
You have eaten _____.
2 He can't move and he can't speak.
He can neither _____.
3 I have two dogs and they sleep in the kitchen.
Both _____.
4 All the children in the class received presents.
Every _____.
5 I asked all the staff but they didn't know the answer.
None _____.
6 Neither David nor I liked the film.
I didn't like the film, and
_____.

7 All the members of the family have keys.
Each member _____.
8 There are no houses in my street without gardens.
Every _____.
9 My bank account is nearly empty.
I have very_____.
10 She said a house was the only thing she wanted.
She said a house was all _____.
11 We are running out of sugar.
We haven't got _____.
12 Alan has a sister, and Brian has a sister.
Both _____.
13 None of the books is missing.
All _____.
14 Few people know about this.
Not _____.
15 She is financially well off.
She has _____.

2 Put a suitable word in each space, or leave the space blank.

1 I went out during the party and bought _____ _____ bottles of beer.
2 When I got into the exam room, I forgot _____.
3 Before the meal began, I put the name of _____ guest on the table.
4 I have very _____ time for watching TV these days.
5 There are _____ _____ people I trust more than you.
6 I couldn't answer the question and _____ could anyone else.
7 He was wounded in _____ legs and lost a lot of blood.
8 I worked overtime _____ day last week and I feel tired.
9 They were _____ suitable _____ cheap enough for us, I'm afraid.
10 I think there is _____ _____ point in wasting any more time.
11 They checked all the hotel rooms, and put extra blankets in _____ one.
12 I won't have time for that, and _____ Peter, I'm afraid.
13 When he met the three sisters, he fell in love with them _____.
14 I saw several films, and enjoyed _____ of them.
15 She was introduced to Graham and Paul, but spoke to _____ of them.

PUNCTUATION

1 *Apostrophe*
The apostrophe is used to indicate that some letters have been left out.
a Letters omitted in writing:
He is = He's
She is not = She isn't
He has = He's
She has not = She hasn't
I will = I'll
I had = I'd
I would = I'd
do not = don't
can not = can't
should not = shouldn't
I am = I'm
You are = You're
They are not = They aren't
I have = I've
They have not = They haven't
I will not = I won't
I had not = I hadn't
I would not = I wouldn't
did not = didn't
could not = couldn't
must not = mustn't
b Some verb forms are shortened in speech but not in writing:
e.g. *should not have*
have is often shortened in speech
c The apostrophe is also used to indicate possession:
Peter's car (of one person)
the boys' uniforms (of more than one)
d Problems
I'd could mean either *I had* or *I would*
its is a possessive form, but has no apostrophe, since *it's* means *it is*

2 *Comma*
Commas separate parts of a sentence, and can be heard as pauses in speech. They are therefore common in lists:
We bought peas, carrots, cabbages, and potatoes
The last comma in such a list is often left out.

Commas may also aid the grammatical meaning:
The passengers, who were tired, fell asleep in the waiting room (all of the passengers)

The passengers who were tired fell asleep in the waiting room (only the ones who were tired) (see Unit 28)

Commas generally also separate clauses linked with *but*:
I ran as fast as I could, but I couldn't catch him
and where a person is called by name, or shouted at:
Pat, where have you been?
Hey, you, what's your name?
Also in time clauses:
As soon as they left, we took down the decorations

3 *Colon and semi-colon*
The colon indicates that what comes next will have the same meaning as what has gone before, and often introduces lists.
I had to buy a large number of things: peas, carrots, etc.

The semi-colon is used as a way of dividing the parts of a complex sentence; or of separating phrases or sentences in a list.
This may be the result of overeating; however, it could also be caused by lack of exercise
I had to buy a large number of things: vegetables for supper; various cleaning things; and some new socks for John

4 *Examples of other punctuation marks*
I met him (and his brother) last year (brackets for a parenthesis)
He was looking into a shop-window (hyphen joins parts of a word)
'Hello,' she said (speech marks at the top of the line, and after any other marks)
We saw 'Hamlet' last night (title)
He said he felt a bit 'grotty' (shows the word is in a different style = slang in this case)

EXERCISES

1 Put the necessary apostrophes in each sentence.
1 My friends arent spending their holidays in hotels.
2 If Id known he wasnt coming Id have invited the twins sister.
3 Some peoples behaviour annoys my fathers friends.
4 Its true that every country has its own beauty.
5 Whos that boy whos carrying my sisters books?

2 Write out each sentence in full.
1 You'd better do it if he's not interested.
2 If I'd seen you I'd have told you.
3 It's no good asking if his brother's got it.
4 I'd rather see if her sisters's still here.
5 Who's taken the apples? They've gone!

3 Put the punctuation given in brackets into each sentence.
1 The last train which was late as usual entered the station. (, ,)
2 At the bottom of the wardrobe there were bundles of old clothes some dirty shoes several empty bags and a pair of skis. (, , ,)
3 When I asked him again I got the same answer no-one had seen her for three days and they didn't expect her back for a week. (, : ,)
4 Nobody had heard of her before in fact they seemed to think I was mad to ask such questions and sent me back to the railway station where I spent another night sitting in the waiting room. (; , , - , -)
5 Hello he said I'm the person who phoned you last night Do you know anything about this girl I asked and took the photo from my pocket. (' , ' , ' . ' ' ? ' ,)

PRONUNCIATION AND SPELLING

1 *The same sound with different spelling*
In each group of words, the parts underlined represent the same sound. Practise saying, and then spelling, each group.

1 suddenly, come, rubbish, love, wonderful, company, mother, flood

2 village, sausage, cabbage, luggage, passage, cottage
Mark the stressed syllables in this group e.g. VILLage

3 listen, castle, whistle, fasten

4 boat, most, coat, home, open, road, code, note, though, know, chose

5 hair, where, stare, share, fairly, there, compare, bear, parents

6 heart, partner, cardboard, fasten, calm, father

7 her, earth, further, word, learn, expert, deserve, hurt

8 now, bough, plough, shout, loud, drown

9 cuff, rough, stuff, enough

10 tomato, about, suggest, forget, perhaps, surprise, autumn, customer, necklace, lemon, open, mother, nature, delicious, thorough, colour
Mark the stressed syllables in this group.

11 position, shame, insurance, relation, precious, ambitious

12 furniture, church, nature, watches

13 confusion, leisure, pleasure, treasure, measure
(This is **not** the sound in *refuse*)

14 wait, weight, great, plate

15 bright, height, despite, site, might

2 *Spelling rules for common problems*
One syllable words ending in one
vowel + one consonant.
swim + ing = swimming
Two syllable words behave in the same way
when the stress is on the second syllable.
begin + ing = beginning
Words which end in vowel + consonant + *e*
do not double but drop the final *e*.
come + ing = coming
Words ending in *-ful* have only one *l*.
wonderful
This ending doubles when *-ly* is added for
adverbs
wonderful + ly = wonderfully

SECTION 2 **VOCABULARY**

TRAVEL, TRANSPORT AND TOURISM

1 Put these words into groups according to topic area. Give each group a title.
Example: ferry, liner, steamer, yacht: Kinds of boat

bicycle	lorry	ambulance
scooter	police car	tractor
double-decker	vintage car	cart
coach	tanker	trolley
sports car	furniture van	tram
taxi	tricycle	caravan
racing car	fire engine	motorbike
carriage	tandem	dustcart

2 Complete each sentence by putting one of the words from Exercise 1, into each space.

1 The injured man was taken to hospital in an _____ .
2 When we went round Scotland by _____ , we found most of the other passengers got on our nerves.
3 They used to collect old unwanted furniture with a horse and _____ .
4 The goods were taken from the port to the factory in a _____ .
5 You get a good view of the sights of a city from the top of a _____ .
6 People who ride _____ are obliged to wear crash-helmets.
7 She likes driving fast in her _____ .
8 The Queen arrived at the cathedral in a beautiful _____ .
9 Since they were thrown out of their cottage they have been living in a _____ .
10 Minutes after she had dialled 999 she saw a/an _____ draw up outside.

3 Match the most suitable endings (a–j) with the beginnings (1-10).

1 She booked a place on a package tour
2 She had bought a return ticket
3 She made an early reservation
4 The flight was cancelled
5 Heavy fog covered the runway
6 The baggage was badly labelled
7 The stewardess asked her to fasten her seat belt
8 Her passport was out of date
9 The customs officer asked her if she had anything to declare
10 There was a two-hour delay

a so she had to sleep in the departure lounge.
b so she put out her cigarette and closed her eyes.
c so she went to the ticket counter and checked her reservation.
d so she arrived at her destination without it.
e so she was refused admission to the departure lounge.
f so she took out her new tape recorder.
g so she didn't have to worry about the travel arrangements.
h so the flight was diverted to Gatwick.
i so she had a look round the duty-free shop.
j so she was certain of a seat on the early flight.

4 Choose the most suitable word in each sentence. (Read all the sentences before starting.)

1 Last year we decided to have a *break/ fortnight/vacancy* in Brighton.
2 We couldn't find a hotel so we stayed in a *boarding-house/pension/cabin.*
3 On the first morning we took some lunch with us and walked down to sit on the *seaside/beach/coast.*
4 It was too cold for swimming so we sat in *deckchairs/armchairs/easy chairs.*
5 There were some children *piloting/ navigating/rowing* a boat.
6 Suddenly a huge *water/wave/rush* knocked them all into the water.
7 The other people soon *aided/rescued/ assisted* them.
8 Luckily none of them was *suffocated/ strangled/drowned.*
9 They were all wet through, but they were all wearing *safety belts/life jackets/ waterproofs.*
10 They ran up and down on the *sand/place/ soil* and were soon dry.

SHOPPING AND MONEY

5 Write the answer to each clue in the blanks below. When you have all the answers, find one other word *down* which means:
a person who walks in the street

```
1    _ _ _|_|_ _ _
2    _ _ _|_|_ _ _
3  _ _ _ _|_|_ _ _ _
4    _ _ _|_|_ _ _
5    _ _ _|_|_ _
6  _ _ _ _|_|_ _
7    _ _ _|_|_ _ _ _
8 _ _ _ _|_|_ _ _ _ _
9  _ _ _ _|_|_ _ _
10 _ _ _ _|_|_ _ _ _ _
```

1 A safe place to leave your car
2 Not in both directions in this street
3 Break this and the police might stop you
4 Where you should walk in the street
5 Useful for going over the road
6 Where roads meet
7 Ask for these if you're lost
8 Stop here if they are red
9 A circular place where roads meet
10 Gives you permission to drive

6 For each word given, circle any word(s) following which help explain it.
Example: **campsite** place person time
(you circle *place*).

1 *voyage* land sea air
2 *set out* leave arrive stop
3 *ride* horse bicycle plane
4 *get on* horse boat car
5 *journey* time long person
6 *arrive* happen reach get to
7 *trip* business short help
8 *get in* boat car plane

Now complete these sentences using one of the words above.

1 A car drew up, a door opened, and a voice told me to _____ .
2 I went to Birmingham on a business _____ .
3 If we want to get there early, we'll have to _____ before 9.
4 She _____ her motorbike, started the engine, and left.
5 They said the ship should _____ at about three this afternoon.
6 Their _____ across Africa took them more than a year.
7 I learned to _____ a bicycle when I was four.
8 The *Titanic* sank on its very first _____ .

1 Fill each space in the sentences with a word formed from *sell* or *sale*.

1 I bought this coat at half price in the _____ .
2 Lots of the cakes were bought, but the small ones were left _____ .
3 Oh dear, there aren't any tickets; tonight is completely _____ out.
4 I see that the house next door is for _____ again.
5 She became a very successful _____ and earned a lot of money.

2 Which products are sold where? Match items from list A with the correct place in list B. (Not all the places in B sell things.)

A	B
cabbages	newsagent's
jigsaws	off licence
whisky	toy shop
rolls	fishmonger's
mince	baker's
cigarettes	hardware store
baked beans	roundabout
stamps	butcher's
chops	town hall
tickets	chemist's
saucepans	bookshop
loaves	station
rolls of film	greengrocer's
nails	library
paperbacks	grocer's
magazines	post office
kippers	
medicine	
bananas	

3 Choose the most suitable word in each sentence.

1 Excuse me, how much do you *charge/cost/sell* to repair shoes?
2 After I had paid, the assistant handed me the *bill/price/receipt*.
3 These trousers cost £10; they were a real *bargain/discount/cheap*.
4 Good morning. Can I *serve/order/help* you?
5 I only have a £20 note. I don't have any *change/rest/money*.
6 This dress I bought here last week is too small. Can I *alter/change/exchange* it?
7 I had to *line/attend/queue* for ages at the check-out desk.
8 Some people find it hard to tell whether fish is *ripe/fresh/new*.
9 I'm afraid those shoes are out of stock at the moment, but we can *order/bring/reserve* them for you if you like.

4 Match the most suitable answers (a–j) with the questions (1–10).

1 Does that seem to be a good fit?
2 How would you like to pay?
3 Shall I wrap it for you?
4 Would you like to try another pair?
5 How about these blue ones?
6 And what can I do for you, sir?
7 Do you want it delivered?
8 Which one is it going to be, then?
9 What size exactly?
10 Is a pound and a half too much?
11 Any particular colour?
12 Did you place an order?

a About eight and a half.
b No, I'll take it with me.
c It is really, yes.
d It doesn't matter much.
e Yes, the name is N. Burton.
f Have you got them in red.
g Is a cheque alright?
h No, I'm not keen on those.
i I'll take it as it is.
j Do you sell shoe-laces?
k This green one, I think.
l Yes, very comfortable.

5 Put a suitable preposition in each space.

1 I asked whether I could pay _____ cheque.
2 They told me they could only deliver if I paid _____ advance.
3 After buying so many things for the house, I ended up _____ debt.
4 While I was in Naples _____ business, I bought this painting.
5 I'm afraid that particular record isn't _____ stock at the moment.
6 Mr Burton-Roberts' book is _____ sale despite the government ban.
7 I'm afraid we'll have to charge you _____ the repairs.
8 There's a considerable shortage _____ good shops in this town.
9 I made _____ a cheque but put the wrong name on it.
10 Noel had to pay _____ the presents after Violet left in a hurry.

6 Read the definitions and guess which word is being defined. The words are listed below, but the letters are mixed up.

nivgass	exast	balle
quceeh	efas	untreco
ramagen	narbd	whelstros
atenugera		

1 Made of paper and used instead of money.
2 The table which a shop assistant stands behind.
3 A kind of box where money is put for protection.
4 Having no value at all.
5 Found inside clothes with washing instructions, etc.
6 Name of a kind of product, e.g. cigarettes.
7 Money which you leave in the bank for a rainy day!
8 Given with goods as a promise of good quality.
9 Money we pay to the government.
10 The person in charge of a large shop.

7 Match the products in A with the shapes or containers in B. Some are possible more than once.

A		B
toothpaste	chocolate	bar
beer	baked beans	box
cigarettes	bananas	tin
sugar	instant coffee	jar
matches	coal	bag
soap	flowers	tube
milk	chocolates	packet
		bottle
		bunch

8 Put a suitable form of these words into each space:
afford charge cost rise pay
economise reduce owe sell

1 I _____ the bank so much that I couldn't take a holiday abroad.
2 When I _____ the rent, I felt as if I had been robbed.
3 I paid in cash and they didn't _____ me so much.
4 After I had _____ my house, I realised I had made a mistake.
5 We _____ so that we could buy a new fridge.
6 The cost of living keeps _____ all the time.
7 We only _____ last year's holiday by cutting down on luxuries.
8 How much did a double room _____?
9 The shop on the corner has _____ everything by fifty per cent.

SPORT AND LEISURE

1 Divide these sports into:
Team Games   Games for Two   Solo Sports
Some may fit into more than one category.

swimming	tennis	squash
sailing	riding	basketball
skiing	football	windsurfing
jogging	cycling	boxing

2 What equipment from this list might you need for the sports in Exercise 1 above?

gloves	boots	watch
shorts	racquet	goggles
helmet	ball	saddle
tracksuit	lifejacket	net

3 Choose the most suitable word in each sentence.

1 Last Saturday Manchester United managed to *beat/win/play* Everton.
2 I'm afraid we'll have to *cancel/wait/postpone* our walk until Tuesday.
3 At the end, the score was 100–100, so the teams *won/drew/equalled*.
4 I've *planned/arranged/supposed* to go jogging with Sue tomorrow.
5 I don't really enjoy *playing/doing/performing* team games.
6 Although our team *failed/missed/lost* the match, we enjoyed it.
7 We had a really good *match/game/competition* of tennis yesterday.
8 I didn't *take/win/succeed* the race, but I did my best.

4 Choose a person from those given below to match these definitions. (Not all are possible.)

referee	seaman	captain
leader	team	audience
champion	chief	group
director	supporters	spectators
trainer	trainer	hooligans
congregation	tutor	lifeguard

1 Someone who helps you when you are in trouble in the sea.
2 Someone who teaches a sportsman or woman how to improve.
3 People who watch others play.
4 Someone who plays in the team and gives orders.
5 Someone who makes the players obey the rules.
6 People who play together.
7 People who cheer their own team.
8 Someone who has performed best in a sport.

5 Put a suitable preposition in each space.

1 Whenever I go _____ a walk, I like to end up in a pub!
2 The secret of jogging is not to be _____ a hurry.
3 After I reached the finishing line I was completely _____ of breath.
4 I realised I was unfit once when I had to run _____ a bus.
5 It is important to stop sometimes _____ a rest.
6 I'm getting better _____ playing golf.
7 She was prevented _____ running fast by the rain.
8 I enjoyed skiing _____ _____ a point; but I don't really like it.
9 Patrick is very keen _____ football and squash.
10 I don't like getting involved _____ organised sport.

6 In each sentence make a word to fill the space, using the word given.

1 At weekends I need some _____ . **RELAX**
2 In my spare time I like to take part in sporting _____ . **ACTIVE**
3 I feel very _____ unless I have some kind of hobby. **BORE**
4 You don't need any special _____ to collect bottles. **KNOW**
5 John found that _____ was an expensive hobby. **PHOTOGRAPH**
6 At the end of the race everyone congratulated the _____ . **WIN**
7 Most sports are rather _____ if you run about a lot. **EXHAUST**
8 I learned that my stamp collection was _____ valuable. **EXPECTED**
9 We couldn't go skating because the lake wasn't _____ . **FREEZE**
10 The exhibition was interesting but lacked _____ . **ORGANISE**

7 Group these words into four word fields.

pastime   weekends   interest
leisure   fascinating   relaxing
hobby   difficult   free time
interesting   activity   demanding
complicated   spare time   time consuming

8 Match the descriptions with the activities. Choose from the activities listed below. (Not all are possible.)

eating in restaurants   football
skiing   cooking
diving   athletics
photography   gardening
car-repairs   stamp-collecting
dressmaking   sailing
walking   parachuting
singing in a choir
arguing

1 You need an album, lots of letters, and a catalogue.
2 You need strong boots, a map, and determination.
3 You need spanners, some knowledge, and patience.
4 You need a fork, a spade and muscles.
5 You need a costume, deep water, and courage.
6 You need snow, special equipment, and some lessons.
7 You need a good voice and some knowledge of music.
8 You need a boat, a wind and a life-jacket.
9 You need some ingredients, a recipe, and a cooker.
10 You need a needle, some thread and some material.

9 Match each object in A, with a verb in B.

A

needle	ticket
stamp	oven
flag	map
camera	piano
ball	spade
spanner	boat

B

take	bake
stick	read
sew	buy
play	kick
wave	dig
turn	sail

Now complete the sentences with a suitable noun and verb from the lists. (Note: change tenses where necessary.)

1 The mechanic took the _____ and _____ the nut until it came loose.
2 I quickly picked up my _____ and _____ a photograph.

3 I was going to _____ on this button but I couldn't find a _____ .
4 I got the _____ from the shed and started to _____ the flowerbed.
5 I put the cake in the _____ but I _____ it for too long.
6 I can't _____ a _____ when I'm driving so I often get lost.
7 The _____ I bought wouldn't _____ on the envelope.
8 As she passed the finishing line, the official _____ a _____ .

HOUSE AND CONTENTS

1 Complete each sentence by putting one of the words into each space.

washbasin   tap   record-player
library   rug   wallpaper
cooker   curtains   shelf
stool   cook   carpet
landing   stove   dining-room
cellar   oven   dishwasher
cupboard   radiator

1 The light is very strong; why don't you pull the _____ .
2 Be careful, that _____ near the bed is very hot.
3 I have to go out, because I need to borrow a book from the _____ .
4 Do you think you could turn down the _____ ? It's very loud.
5 Put the loaves in the _____ and bake them until they go brown.
6 I can't stand flowery _____ ; why don't we paint the room white?
7 At the top of the stairs, there's a door at the end of the _____ .
8 There's a small _____ on the floor so your feet will be warm.
9 There isn't any soap on the _____ ; can I have some please?
10 We keep coal down in the _____ and bring it up when we need it.
11 She knows a lot of recipes and is a very good _____ .
12 I keep some of my books on a _____ above my bed.
13 There weren't any chairs but the little boy sat on a low _____ .
14 Put all the dirty knives and forks in the _____ , would you?
15 When it was time for lunch we all went into the _____ .
16 The floor was covered with a bright green wall-to-wall _____ .
17 I've decided to buy a new electric _____ to replace my old one.
18 In the middle of the hut was an old _____ which burned wood.
19 The _____ in the bathroom was dripping and kept me awake.
20 Put everything back in the _____ when you've finished, please.

2 Complete each sentence by putting one of the words into each space.

ceiling   cushion   washing-machine
stairs   gate   sink
desk   doormat   attic
three-piece suite   fridge   shutters
dressing table   greenhouse   blind
roof   settee   central heating
bookcase   balcony

1 Put that plate of food straightaway into the _____ .
2 There were Christmas decorations hanging from the _____ .
3 She manages to grow tropical fruit in her _____ in the garden.
4 The three of them sat on the _____ trying to drink their tea.
5 She sat at the _____ putting on make up and combing her hair.
6 Could you wipe your dirty feet on the _____ before you come in?
7 Now I work at home instead of at the office, I've bought a _____ .
8 After the high winds, the rain started coming through their _____ .
9 We put all our old things in the _____ at the top of the house.
10 If you put the curtains in the _____ they may be damaged.
11 During the storm, we closed the _____ to protect the windows.
12 There is only enough room here for three chairs, not for a _____ .
13 The postman never shuts the _____ when he leaves the garden.
14 They stepped out onto the _____ to watch the crowds below.
15 The _____ system in this block of flats doesn't keep us warm.
16 The sun was very strong, so I let down the _____ .
17 She fell down the _____ , but luckily was not hurt.
18 That chair must be uncomfortable; have this _____ .
19 Those shelves aren't strong enough; we'll have to get a _____ .
20 Put all the dirty cups and saucers in the _____ please.

3 Match the types of houses (a–j) with the details (1–10) which follow. Several details go with each type of house.

a cottage
b high-rise block
c detached house
d flat
e bungalow
f semi-detached house
g terraced house

1 in the country
2 a row of houses joined together
3 two houses joined together
4 one floor only
5 in the city
6 in a suburb
7 a very tall building with flats
8 a house standing on its own
9 perhaps with a lift
10 with a garden.

4 Match the things in A with the rooms in B. More than one answer is sometimes possible.

A	B
cooker	sitting room
dressing table	kitchen
pillow	bathroom
settee	hall
sink	bedroom
coffee-table	
armchair	
bunks	
doormat	
washbasin	
wardrobe	
bookcase	
cupboard	
fridge	
eiderdown	
rocking-chair	

5 Choose the most suitable word in each sentence.

1 We sat and had tea under a tall shady *bush/tree*.
2 A small *road/path* leads to the bottom of the garden.
3 I must go and cut the *lawn/hedge*; we can't see over it.
4 Don't forget to shut the garden *door/gate* when you leave.
5 There is an old wooden *fence/wall* between the two gardens.
6 We keep the tools in a little *cottage/shed* in the garden.
7 I must remember to *wet/water* the flowers before I go.
8 She said she would *plant/grow* the tomatoes on Sunday.
9 If you have time, could you *dig/bury* this flowerbed?
10 The *grass/grasses* in the garden *is/are* too long.
11 He decided to *pick up/pick* all the apples from the old tree.
12 If you are going to repair the roof, you'll need *scales/a ladder*.
13 During the storm, the wind blew down the *chimney/fireplace*.
14 Some *bricks/tiles* fell from the roof and now water gets in.
15 I have to get the TV *antenna/aerial* repaired as well.
16 She put the plant on the window *shelf/sill* so it was in the sun.
17 The postman put the postcard through our *letter box/post box*.
18 I've left the car outside in the *parking/drive*.
19 Can you put this rubbish outside in the *wastepaper basket/dustbin*?
20 She leant her bike against a *lighthouse/lamp-post*.
21 Our dog has a *hut/kennel* just like Snoopy.
22 The *drain/sink* outside is completely blocked with leaves.
23 He went to get some *earth/ground* for the indoor plants.
24 A large *trunk/branch* fell from the tree during the night.
25 You are not supposed to park on the *footpath/pavement*.

WORK

1 Match the names of jobs in A, with the tools/equipment used in B. More than one answer may be possible.

A	B
mechanic	tray
doctor	brush
teacher	rifle
painter	spanner
dustman	net
farmer	spade
waiter	instrument
dentist	thermometer
hairdresser	whistle
postman	dustbin
musician	broom
soldier	tape measure
fisherman	scissors
gardener	typewriter
electrician	bicycle
tailor	calculator
carpenter	drill
fireman	spoon
miner	blackboard
cleaner	tractor
accountant	screwdriver
cook	saw
police officer	hosepipe
secretary	lamp

2 Put one of the following words, or a word formed from it in each space:
work   business   job.

1 Why are you telling me that? It's none of your _____ .
2 I missed the bus and I was half an hour late for _____ .
3 They gave her a copy of the collected _____ of Shakespeare.
4 The company sent three _____ to repair the damaged roof.
5 I lost my _____ because the factory I was working in closed down.
6 At the moment, there are over a million people out of _____ .
7 Their company was bought by a very rich young _____ .
8 I've built a small _____ in my garage, and I do car repairs.
9 It was a difficult _____ , but we managed to fix the bike in the end.
10 I had a lot of _____ to do, but I finished them eventually.

3 Complete each sentence by putting one of the words into each space.

experience   wages   interview
notice   references   promotion
applications   salary   resignation
qualifications

1 The workmen collected their _____ every Friday afternoon.
2 He did well in his job and was given _____ .
3 We'll employ you if you have good _____ from previous jobs.
4 _____ should be sent to the manager at the address below.
5 My boss gave me a week's _____ that the firm no longer needed me.
6 Your _____ will increase by 15% every year.
7 You have a diploma, but you don't have enough _____ for this job.
8 I was so annoyed by her attitude that I handed in my _____ .
9 Successful applicants must attend an/a _____ .
10 What kind of _____ for this job have you got?

4 Match the tools and equipment below with the descriptions of what each is used for in 1 to 25.

hammer	crane	tape-recorder
spade	screwdriver	file
spanner	drill	pliers
scissors	wheelbarrow	axe
net	pump	calculator
saw	computer	telex
lawnmower	ruler	hosepipe
broom	tractor	brush
ladder		

1 for cutting grass
2 for pulling machinery on a farm
3 for making holes in wood or stone
4 for cutting wood accurately
5 for mathematical problems
6 for delivering water
7 for sweeping floors, etc.
8 for lifting heavy weights
9 for measuring lengths, etc.
10 for sending written messages
11 for cutting wood in rough shapes
12 for cutting paper or cloth
13 for climbing up walls, etc.
14 for carrying things a short way
15 for copying voices or music
16 for storing information
17 for smoothing surfaces
18 for turning screws

19 for cutting or bending wire
20 for hitting nails
21 for digging holes
22 for catching fish
23 for making air or water move
24 for turning nuts and bolts
25 for putting on paint

5 Who would you need in each of the following situations? Choose from the list of people below.

a vet	an accountant	a librarian
a social worker	a caterer	an estate agent
a carpenter	a mechanic	a vicar
a secretary	an electrician	a plumber
a decorator	an architect	a solicitor

1 Water is leaking from the pipes in your bathroom.
2 You have a lot of letters to write and appointments you forget.
3 You have no idea how much you have earned or how much tax you owe.
4 Your dog is limping after hurting its leg.
5 You own a small piece of land and would like to build a house on it.
6 Your lights keep going out for no reason.
7 You have terrible problems at home and don't know what to do.
8 You want to sell your house and buy a new one in another town.
9 You would like to get married in your local church.
10 You want to borrow a rare book on medieval history.
11 You are giving a party for a hundred people and need some food.
12 Your house badly needs painting and a change of wallpaper.
13 You need some new wooden shelves and can't make them yourself.
14 You get a letter threatening to take you to court because of a debt.
15 Your car makes terrible noises and then refuses to start.

6 Choose the most suitable word in each sentence.

1 I wanted to work less so I took a *part-time/full-time* job.
2 The trouble with my job is that it has no *promotion/prospects*.
3 Last summer for two weeks I took a *temporary/part-time* job.
4 Working in a factory can be very *bored/boring*.
5 I read about the job in an *advertisement/announcement*.
6 She was told that the job *wanted/needed* more experience.
7 The company increased sales and made a larger *salary/profit*.
8 The secretary stole *a considerable/an extensive* sum from the safe.
9 Could I make *an appointment/a date* to see the manager
10 The firm closed down because of *economical/economic* difficulties.
11 They paid him £50 each week for his *extra time/overtime*.
12 Japanese managers wear *uniforms/overalls* just like the workers.

FOOD AND EATING

1 Complete each sentence by putting one of the words into each space.

menu	prescription	recipe
warm up	receipt	meals
plate	requested	rare
overdone	table-cloth	ordered
fried	ingredients	cork
course	café	recommend
cover	bottle	boiled
book	cafeteria	tip
burn		

1 The waitress asked them if they had _____ any food.
2 They didn't know what there was to eat so they asked for the _____ .
3 That restaurant is very popular and so you have to _____ a table.
4 The waiter was slow and very rude so they didn't leave a _____ .
5 I spilled the wine on the table and the waiter brought a clean _____ .
6 When she opened the champagne, the _____ flew across the room.
7 I like my steak _____, you know, really red and soft.
8 In some restaurants, they _____ food which has been pre-cooked.
9 I like to drink water with all my _____, including breakfast.
10 We enjoyed the dish so much that we asked the chef for the _____ .
11 When I tried to cook the dish at home, I didn't have all the _____ .
12 I like a _____ egg for breakfast, cooked for 3½ minutes exactly.
13 I didn't know what to have so I asked the waiter to _____ something.
14 The first _____ was so filling that I lost my appetite.
15 We stopped and had breakfast in a small roadside _____ .

2 Choose the most suitable word in each sentence.

1 Boil the potatoes in plenty of water in a *saucepan/frying pan*.
2 They gave me a cup of tea, but the *plate/saucer* was cracked.
3 He put the sugar in his coffee and *mixed/stirred* it with a spoon.
4 She offered me a slice of her freshly-baked chocolate *cake/sweet*.
5 He *roasted/baked* the joint of beef in the oven for two hours.
6 For breakfast every morning she has coffee and a *toast/sandwich*.
7 The worst part of cooking is the *washing/washing up* afterwards.
8 Leave the biscuits in the oven until they are *made/done*.
9 It is handy to keep some *freezing/frozen* food in the fridge.
10 He went to the baker's and bought two fresh *loaves/breads*.
11 I left the milk on the gas too long and it boiled *over/off*.
12 I threw the bread away because it was *rotten/stale*.
13 She *squeezed/squashed* two oranges and drank the juice.
14 We served the salad in a large decorated *plate/dish*.
15 He put the lamb on the table and *chopped/carved* it into slices.

3 Complete each sentence in the most suitable way by putting one of the words into each space.

chops	potatoes	fish
beef	salad	cheese
lemon	plums	cream
eggs	mushrooms	butter
pepper	onions	cucumber

1 Every morning for breakfast she eats scrambled _____ .
2 Put the sauce on the pizza and add some chopped _____ .
3 Spaghetti is more tasty if you add grated _____ .
4 When I was on a diet I was allowed to eat only grilled _____ .
5 With my steak, I ordered a mixed _____ .
6 The fish was served with a thin slice of _____ .
7 He enjoys sandwiches which contain slices of roast _____ .
8 In the summer I love eating dishes of strawberries and _____ .
9 I went out to the garden to dig up some more _____ .
10 She likes her bread to be spread thickly with _____ .
11 I made the sandwiches from thin slices of peeled _____ .

12 At the back of the house is a tree laden with ripe _____ .
13 I asked the butcher to give me three large _____ .
14 She didn't eat the hamburger because it smelled of _____ .
15 He started sneezing as soon as he shook the _____ .

4 Make the names of fruit and vegetables from the letters given.

1 sape	8 hecap	15 pergas
2 pergrufita	9 arpe	16 prutin
3 cultete	10 egarno	17 mootat
4 slump	11 oboteter	18 snabe
5 pleap	12 anaban	19 fuelailcrow
6 lipanpeep	13 tracor	20 psyrabrer
7 clarig	14 bagbace	

5 Match the most suitable endings (a–j) with the beginnings (1–10).

1 I ordered a plate of mushroom soup
2 I went up to the bar and asked for
3 I washed and peeled the potatoes
4 I didn't like the cheese
5 The waiter brought me
6 I broke both the eggs
7 The dessert looked fattening
8 Stir the mixture slowly
9 I tasted the orange
10 Turn down the gas
11 I ate too many chocolates
12 There were no fresh vegetables
13 I didn't feel very hungry
14 Wash the dried beans thoroughly
15 She picked all the strawberries

a as it was too strong for me.
b and beat them in a bowl.
c but it was rotten.
d until the butter melts.
e when the milk begins to boil.
f and lost my appetite.
g as a first course.
h so I didn't have potatoes.
i and leave them in water.
j two pints of bitter.
k a small stale roll.
l so I had fruit instead.
m and made them into jam.
n because of the strike.
o and cut them into slices.

6 Choose the most suitable verb in each sentence.

1 Put the spaghetti in the water when it begins to *heat/boil/steam*.
2 *Grill/fry/boil* the slices of meat in plenty of oil for one minute.
3 *Chop/slice/carve* the onions into small pieces and add to the butter.
4 *Roast/bake/cook* the bread in a medium oven until it turns brown.
5 When the butter *dissolves/melts/runs* add the sugar and the cocoa.
6 *Peel/clean/skin* the potatoes and cut them into slices.
7 Bring to the boil, *shaking/stirring/moving* gently until it thickens.
8 She *poured/tipped/sliced* the cream from the jug into the bowls.
9 Oh dear! I'm afraid I've *roasted/burned/grilled* the toast.
10 Before adding the tea, *boil/heat/warm* the pot with a little water.
11 *Sink/soak/wash* dried vegetables for at least ten hours.
12 Please *give/serve/help* yourself to another portion.
13 She *destroyed/collapsed/spoiled* the soup by adding too much salt.
14 I find it difficult to *judge/measure/weigh* how much salt to use.
15 If it cooks too quickly, *turn up/turn out/turn down* the gas a little.

HEALTH, FITNESS AND THE BODY

1 Complete this word puzzle. All the words are connected with health.

— P — — —		One of these each day keeps away the doctor.
— — L —		White and refreshing, and good for you.
— — E — —		White or brown, could be fattening.
— — — N — — — — — —		Exercises to make you fit and strong.
— — — — T — — — — —		You'll be healthy if you eat this. (two words)
— Y — — — — —		A way to get fit on two wheels.
— — — — O — — — —		Obey this sign and you'll breathe easily.
— — F — — —		Do this when your friends offer you sweets.
— — — E — —		Eight hours of this does you good.
— — — — X — — — — —		Don't suffer from stress; enjoy this.
— — E —		Go on one if you are overweight.
— R — — — —		Eat one if you need vitamin C.
— — — C — — — —		Have it at the doctor's to see if you are fit (two words).
— — I —		Not thin, and definitely not fat.
— — — S — — — —		Breathe this and feel healthy. (two words)
E — — — — —		If you are fit, you have a lot of this.

2 Complete each sentence by putting one of the words into each space.

wrist	thumb	throat
ankles	heels	tongue
knee	toe	cheeks
shoulder	elbow	waist
forehead	neck	chest

1 After giving her speech, she had a sore _____ and couldn't talk.
2 I'm getting fat and my trousers don't fit me round the _____ .
3 I looked at the watch on his _____ and saw that it was time to go.
4 When I play tennis, sweat runs down my _____ and into my eyes.
5 She dropped the chair on her foot and hurt her big _____ .
6 The doctor told me to open my mouth and put out my _____ .
7 My new shoes were too tight and gave me blisters on my _____ .
8 There was a sleeping bag hanging on a strap from his _____ .
9 I had bronchitis so the doctor took an X-ray of my _____ .
10 She was wearing a long skirt which reached down to her _____ .
11 The president greeted the minister by kissing him on both _____ .
12 I fell while playing football and twisted my _____ .
13 When she was a baby, she always had her _____ in her mouth.
14 I don't like wearing a tie because it feels too tight round my _____ .
15 Please don't lean your _____ on the table while you're eating.

3 Match the most suitable endings (a–j) with the beginnings (1–10).

1 The doctor wrote a prescription
2 I had to take the tablets
3 I thought I had a temperature
4 I put a plaster on my finger
5 I lost a lot of weight
6 The nurse rolled up my sleeve
7 I took an aspirin
8 I had a bad cough
9 I broke my arm and they put it
10 I slipped down the stairs
11 I broke my leg
12 I was feeling very depressed
13 I phoned the surgery
14 My foot felt very sore
15 I dialled 999

a because it was bleeding badly.
b and my headache disappeared.
c in plaster for several weeks.
d and they gave me an X-ray.
e a sore throat and a temperature.
f and the doctor helped me a lot.
g and I took it to the chemist's.
h and the ambulance soon arrived.
i and I borrowed a thermometer.
j and gave me an injection.
k and I rubbed ointment on it.
l and badly twisted my ankle.
m three times a day after meals.
n and made an appointment.
o after going on a special diet.

4 Complete each sentence by putting one of the words into each space.

injection	diet	fattening
sick	tired	exercises
medicine	energy	appointment
tiring	temperature	fit
unhealthy	pills	exercise

1 The doctor told me I should take more _____.

2 I was overweight so I decided to go on a _____.

3 Every morning before breakfast I do some _____.

4 I didn't feel well so I decided to take my _____.

5 I was in severe pain and had to have an _____.

6 I took up gymnastics because I wanted to feel _____.

7 Most people agree that smoking is very _____.

8 Whenever I eat too much I feel rather _____.

9 In order to see the doctor I had to have an _____.

10 I had to give up jogging because it made me feel _____.

11 You won't get better by taking too much _____.

12 After giving up smoking I found I had more _____.

13 I like health food best because it isn't very _____.

14 When I first started cycling I found it very _____.

15 Every day I had to take several _____.

5 Match the noun (a–i) with the description of its use (1–9).

a for putting on a small cut
b for taking your temperature with
c for moving ill people who are sitting down
d for cleaning the skin with
e for carrying people who are lying down
f for cleaning your teeth with
g for putting on sore parts of the skin
h for taking injured or ill people to hospital
i for wrapping round injured parts of the body

1	stretcher	6	cotton wool
2	ambulance	7	wheelchair
3	bandage	8	toothbrush
4	plaster	9	thermometer
5	ointment		

6 Choose a suitable word or phrase used in this unit to fill each space.

1 If you feel _____, then you should think about dieting.
2 It is important to clean your _____ after every meal.
3 I sneezed four times, and later started to _____ loudly.
4 After I heard the bad news I felt very _____ for a while.
5 Three people were _____ in the accident and taken to hospital.
6 I woke up in the night with a severe _____ in my knee.
7 While I was cooking the dinner I _____ myself badly with a knife.
8 I decided to stop working in the evenings because it was too _____.
9 When the nurse gave me the _____ I hardly felt it at all.
10 He broke his _____ playing football, and couldn't write for a month.
11 The doctor put a _____ on her arm, and fastened it with a safety-pin.
12 After walking all day in my new shoes, I had _____ feet.
13 She was worried because her cut leg wouldn't stop _____.
14 I had a headache, a temperature and a sore _____, so I went to bed.
15 She advised me to _____ sugar in my tea if I wanted to lose weight.

CHARACTER, APPEARANCE AND CLOTHES

1 Complete each sentence by putting one of the words into each space.

skirt	jacket	jeans
trousers	suit	scarf
pullover	belt	gloves
stockings	socks	blouse
shorts	shirt	overcoat

1 It was such a cold day that I wore a long woolly _____ round my neck.
2 His _____ had holes in them because his shoes were too tight.
3 When he was ten, he went to school for the first time in long _____ .
4 I had my _____ on, and so I couldn't hold the pen properly.
5 She bought a new silk _____ with large white buttons.
6 In my office, most men wear a white _____ and a tie.
7 She caught her new _____ on the desk and had to put on a new pair.
8 When it's hot, I usually wear just a T-shirt and a pair of _____ .
9 He was wearing a long _____ , and carrying a rolled umbrella.
10 If you don't wear a _____ , your trousers might fall down!
11 She was sent home from school because her _____ was far too short.
12 He took off his leather _____ , and hung it up behind the door.
13 She decided to wear an old pair of _____ when she painted the house.
14 He had on a v-necked _____ , and a pair of white trousers.
15 If you wear a dark _____ , people think you look like a manager.

2 Complete each sentence by putting one of the adjectives into each space.

reliable	mean	patient
punctual	nervous	cautious
generous	miserable	brave
honest	ashamed	sympathetic
annoying	determined	grateful

1 Someone who is willing to wait without getting angry is _____ .
2 Someone who thanks you for something you did is _____ .
3 Someone whose habits make you feel a little angry is _____ .
4 Someone who is very worried before an important exam is _____ .
5 Someone who is willing to understand your problems is _____ .
6 Someone who does not like to spend money is _____ .
7 Someone who feels unhappy because they did a wrong thing is _____ .
8 Someone who is always on time is _____ .
9 Someone who refuses to give up is _____ .
10 Someone who risks their life to save another person is _____ .
11 Someone who always does what they say is _____ .
12 Someone who feels very unhappy is _____ .
13 Someone who gives back the money they find is _____ .
14 Someone who often pays for all their friends is _____ .
15 Someone who is very careful before doing something is _____ .

3 Find the error in each sentence and correct it.

1 She was dressing in a long black dress and having on a hat.
2 The shoes were not fitting me, so I didn't buy them.
3 He was wearing a new grey trouser and a white blouse.
4 His new green and blue pullover didn't really suit him very much.
5 I use to wear casual clothes to work, not formal clothes.
6 I tried on the shoes, but they were the wrong number for me.
7 I get up at 7, wear my clothes, have breakfast and then leave.
8 I liked the red shoes, but they didn't suit my dress.
9 He bought a new dark blue costume for the wedding.
10 In the summer he usually wears short-sleeved shirts.
11 Her new jean was a bit too small so she changed it.
12 All policemen wear costumes so that they can be recognised.
13 In the winter he wears long woolly stockings to keep warm.
14 These feel very straight; do you have a larger pair?
15 In this photo, the man wears shorts and a T-shirt.

4 Complete each sentence by putting one of the verbs into each space.

laughed whispered sneezed
shouted talked spoke
cried yawned smiled
screamed

1 He was so tired that he _____ all through the lesson.
2 When she put the pepper on her food she suddenly _____ .
3 The two friends _____ their secrets to each other in the corner.
4 He _____ at her, and then wished her good morning.
5 When the little boy hurt his leg, he _____ until his mother came.
6 When we met again after so many years, we _____ for hours on end.
7 They _____ at him to go away, but he took no notice.
8 I _____ so much when I saw that comedy film, that I couldn't stop.
9 She _____ very softly so it was difficult to hear what she said.
10 As soon as I saw the snake, I _____, and jumped on a chair.

5 Complete each sentence by putting one of the words into each space.

angry fashionable bored
friendly jealous polite
silly lazy lonely
depressed strict upset
interested rude careless

1 I live on my own but I don't really feel _____ .
2 When she saw him with another girl she felt really _____ .
3 I think that people who interrupt all the time are _____ .
4 When they told her the bad news she was very _____ .
5 Check your work again and try not to be so _____ .
6 There is nothing to do in this town and I feel _____ .
7 Our new neighbours are so helpful and are really _____ .
8 She needs someone to cheer her up because she feels so _____ .
9 He just does nothing all day, and is really _____ .

10 When you talk to customers, try to be more _____ .
11 When I tried to explain he shouted and became _____ .
12 I think you are being childish and rather _____ .
13 She learned a lot because she was really _____ .
14 My new boss gives us a lot of orders and is very _____ .
15 She dresses well and her clothes are very _____ .

6 Put the words in each phrase into an order that makes sense.

1 a skirt cotton green long
2 striped red silk blue pyjamas and
3 girl hair with tall long a black
4 socks thick long woollen
5 necked sweater blue polo a
6 new trousers blue pair of a
7 shoes heeled black high
8 short shirt best my sleeved
9 brown her shoes old leather
10 a feather hat it in with a

ENTERTAINMENT AND THE ARTS

1 Complete each sentence by putting one of the words into each space.

performance	scenery	part
interval	act	applause
cast	critic	review
stage		

1 It is a difficult play to put on, as it has a _____ of over fifty.
2 At the end of the play the audience burst into _____ .
3 During the _____ , I went to the bar and had a drink.
4 My uncle used to get free theatre tickets because he was a _____ .
5 The _____ was well painted, and really looked like a castle.
6 I'm afraid that tonight's _____ has been cancelled.
7 She was too old for the _____ of Ophelia, but she did her best.
8 The play only had one good _____ , and that was in the local paper.
9 At the end, everyone came on to the _____ and bowed to the audience.
10 Although he has a good speaking voice he can't really _____ well.

2 Put a suitable preposition into each space. Choose from

from   at   to   about   for   in   by   on.

1 I think it would be a good idea to go _____ the cinema.
2 I read about the accident _____ the newspaper.
3 I saw a film about pollution _____ television.
4 I borrowed the book I needed _____ the library.
5 I read about that _____ one of the books I borrowed.
6 My class is putting _____ a play at the end of term.
7 What's _____ at the theatre this week?
8 I thought he acted very well _____ his first film.
9 I can't remember who that book is _____ .
10 He is not nervous when he is actually _____ the stage.
11 Who was the king played _____ ? Was it Laurence Olivier?
12 She was given an Oscar _____ her performance in *Gone With The Wind*.
13 I couldn't see his name _____ the programme.

3 Match the people in A with the activities in B.

A	B
Person	playing records in a disco
director	singing in an opera
novelist	writing poems
journalist	organising a newspaper
clown	introducing TV programmes
soprano	making films
conjuror	writing for a newspaper
editor	making people laugh
conductor	writing stories
disc jockey	doing magic tricks
announcer	directing an orchestra
comedian	working in a circus
poet	

4 Complete each sentence by putting one of the words into each space.

publish	pick up	paint
play	broadcast	advertise
boo	put on	act
report	illustrate	show
applaud	print	make

1 Which company is going to _____ her new novel?
2 I find it difficult to _____ the BBC World Service.
3 He used to _____ portraits but now does mainly landscapes.
4 They are going to _____ the Cup Final live from Wembley.
5 The play was so bad that everyone started to _____ half-way through.
6 On some television channels, no-one is allowed to _____ .
7 A well-known artist is going to _____ Mary's new book.
8 To be a good opera singer, you have to be able to sing and _____ .
9 The violinist stood up and started to _____ some Mozart.
10 They decided to _____ the books in Hong Kong, as it was cheaper.
11 When the dancers finished, the audience began to _____ .
12 Our Drama Club is going to _____ Macbeth this year.
13 The journalist went to _____ on the fighting in Central America.
14 They have decided to _____ a film about the life of Buddy Holly.
15 The cinema opposite has decided to _____ old silent films next week.

5 Arrange these words according to topic area.

cover   introduction   contents
close-up   screen   note
brush   conductor   index
draughts   cards   tune
landscape   pack   model
chess   special effects   chapter
frame   solo   record
director   board   camera
portrait   camera

1 music   2 cinema   3 reading

_____ _____ _____
_____ _____ _____
_____ _____ _____
_____ _____ _____
_____ _____ _____

4 painting   5 home entertainment

_____ _____
_____ _____
_____ _____
_____ _____
_____ _____

6 In each sentence, underline the italicised word or phrase which is *negative* in meaning.

1 The film was *superbly/dreadfully* directed.
2 The play was *gripping/dull* from beginning to end.
3 I couldn't *put the book down/get into the book*.
4 This record will *get nowhere/reach the top*.
5 His acting was *out of this world/beyond belief*.
6 It's the kind of music that *makes you get up/gets you down*.
7 Her painting is *hard on the eye/catches the eye*.
8 That programme *puts me to sleep/doesn't let me sleep*.
9 Their music is *tuneless/tuneful*.
10 The film had *very few characters/very little character*.
11 Her singing *drove everyone wild/made everyone mad*.
12 The scene was *brilliantly filmed/hopelessly filmed*.

SOCIAL AND ENVIRONMENTAL ISSUES

1 Complete each sentence by putting one of the words into each space.

stolen   court   accused
burglar   robbed   fine
arrested   prison   guilty
station

1 She was _____ of taking the purse from the old lady's handbag.
2 Any _____ would be able to open this window and get into the house.
3 It was a serious offence, and he was sent to _____ for two years.
4 The policeman took him to the _____ and asked him some questions.
5 After he had been _____, he immediately phoned the police.
6 Most people who are caught driving too fast have to pay a _____.
7 When they appeared in _____, they denied that they had hit him.
8 All my money was _____, and I had to walk to the nearest village.
9 The jury decided he was not _____, and so he was set free.
10 They were _____ for smashing windows and fighting in the street.

2 Complete each sentence by putting one of the words into each space. More than one answer may be possible.

difficult   exhausted   tiring
dangerous   expensive   busy
common   noisy   polluted
unbearable   crowded   depressing
heavy   worried   lonely

1 People don't get to work on time because the traffic is _____.
2 Many people left the city because the air was so _____.
3 I find public transport uncomfortable because it is so _____.
4 I'm afraid to walk in the city at night because it is _____.
5 Many old people who live alone find life rather _____.
6 Driving in the centre is hard and parking is _____.
7 People who commute to work every day find it _____.
8 In some parts of the city, crime is very _____.
9 Living in the city centre can be very _____.
10 If you live near a main road the noise can be _____.

11 Even in the crowds of the city you can feel _____ .
12 By the time they get home, many commuters are _____ .
13 Because of the crime in cities, many people feel _____ .
14 Living in a flat can be a problem if the neighbours are _____ .
15 No-one seems to have time to stop because they are so _____ .

3 Complete each sentence by putting one of the words into each space.

banned	rebuilt	changed
preserved	widened	built
planted	closed	controlled
destroyed	increased	provided
improved	demolished	planned

1 Unless the road is _____ , the traffic will never move freely.
2 The old houses in bad condition should be _____ .
3 The number of parks should be _____ , so there is more fresh air.
4 Cars should be _____ from the centre, so there is less pollution.
5 Unfortunately, the beautiful parts of the old city are being _____ .
6 Building of new blocks in the city is _____ by the government.
7 Some old buildings have been _____ in their original condition.
8 Thousands of trees have been _____ along the new roads.
9 The ruined castle was _____ , and is now used as a museum.
10 More places in old people's homes will be _____ by our new plan.
11 Traffic conditions have _____ since they built the new road.
12 Little has _____ in this part of the city since the Middle Ages.
13 The new bridge was _____ by a Japanese engineering company.
14 The government _____ to build a motorway, but could not afford it.
15 The road is _____ , because they are building a new subway.

4 Complete each sentence by putting one of the words into each space.

home	court	car park
town hall	orphanage	sports centre
parliament	night school	village hall
club	shopping	market place
nursery school	centre	cathedral
library		

1 Many working mothers send their children to a _____ .
2 On Saturday I go to the supermarket in the new _____ .
3 The New Year dance was held in the _____ .
4 The local fair was held in the _____ .
5 I always go to the morning service in the _____ .
6 The old couple now live in an old people's _____ .
7 She learned to play tennis down at the _____ .
8 I borrowed these books from the local _____ .
9 Last year she was elected to _____ .
10 Most young people go to the youth _____ .
11 He was arrested for shoplifting and had to go to _____ .
12 She managed to pass her exams by going to _____ .
13 When her parents died the child had to go to the _____ .
14 They have just built a new multi-storey _____ .
15 I went to see the mayor in his office at the _____ .

5 Arrange these words according to topic area.

employer	reference	pupil
solicitor	unemployment	election
strike	form	fine
primary	comprehensive	vote
arrest	shift	offence
party	majority	uniform
evidence	demonstration	

1 politics 2 education

_____ _____
_____ _____
_____ _____
_____ _____
_____ _____

3 law 4 work

_____ _____
_____ _____
_____ _____
_____ _____

WORD BUILDING (1)

6 Complete each sentence by putting one of the words from Exercise 5 into each space.

1 The policeman put his hand on my arm and said I was under _____ .
2 Before they gave her the job, they asked for a _____ from her boss.
3 When I was in the third _____ at school, I started learning German.
4 At the last general _____ , the government won another victory.
5 There was a _____ against nuclear weapons in London yesterday.
6 She had to pay a _____ because she didn't have a TV licence.
7 The police kept the knife because it was part of the _____ .
8 The teachers decided to go on _____ because they were badly paid.
9 Children from 5 to 11 go to _____ school.
10 I went to a _____ and asked for some advice about my divorce.
11 She worked on the night _____ at the local plastics factory.
12 As it was her first _____ , she did not receive a heavy punishment.
13 I didn't _____ for her because I didn't agree with her policies.
14 Most children used to wear a _____ to school when I was young.
15 Many people left the country because _____ was so high.

1 Fill the space in each sentence with a word ending in -*ful*.

1 When you go camping, a sharp knife can be very _____ .
2 Her portrait shows that she was a very _____ woman.
3 We had a _____ holiday, and enjoyed every minute of it.
4 Be _____ ! You nearly stepped on my foot!
5 Add one _____ of sugar, and stir thoroughly.

2 Fill the space in each sentence with a word ending in -*ness*.

1 Many old people who live alone suffer from _____
2 We wish you every _____ in your new job.
3 Please be more polite! I can't stand _____ .
4 You've been very good to me. Thank you for your _____ .
5 He never spends a penny on anyone! What dreadful _____ !
6 Isn't this pullover lovely? Feel the _____ of the wool.

3 For each sentence, make a word beginning *un-*, *dis-*, *in-*, *im-*, or *mis-*, using the word given.

1 I'm afraid that I am _____ with your work. — SATISFIED
2 That is not true. It seems that you have been _____ . — LED
3 It is very _____ that she'll come back, in my opinion. — LIKELY
4 That's _____ ! It simply can't be true. — POSSIBLE
5 No, I didn't say that. There seems to be a _____ . — UNDERSTANDING
6 Don't wear a suit, it's going to be an _____ dinner. — FORMAL
7 The children are so _____ . They don't do what I say. — OBEDIENT
8 That's very _____ . As a rule, it rains a lot in July. — USUAL
9 I think it would be _____ not to reply to the letter. — POLITE

10 You must check your work; it's very _____ . ACCURATE

11 Sorry, but I am _____ to lend you my motorbike. WILLING

12 My parents _____ of my staying out so late. APPROVE

13 You've got no ideas! You're very _____ . IMAGINATIVE

14 I was _____ to the sun, and got very sunburned. USED

15 The meal he cooked was completely _____ . EDIBLE

4 Use the italicised word to make a word which can fill the space in the sentence which follows.

1 My work doesn't *satisfy* me at all.
I get no _____ from my work.

2 'Happy Days' was one of the horses in the *lead*.
'Happy Days' was one of the _____ horses.

3 It is not *likely* to snow.
There is no _____ of it snowing.

4 Flying without wings is just not *possible*!
Flying without wings is an _____ .

5 He doesn't like to be *formal*.
He believes in _____ .

6 The point is, will they *obey* him?
The point is whether they will be _____ or not.

7 It would be *polite* to reply.
We don't want to be accused of _____ .

8 I would like a watch which was *accurate*.
The important thing about a watch is its _____ .

9 I would like you to *approve* of what I do.
I would like your _____ for what I do.

10 She is unable to *imagine* anything at all.
She has no _____ .

11 I could see that he was not *willing* to do it.
I could see his _____ .

12 He wasn't *strong* enough to lift the table alone.
He didn't have the _____ to lift the table alone.

13 This country is *short* of natural resources.
In this country there is a _____ of natural resources.

14 They could not prevent the complete *destruction* of the city.
They could not prevent the city being completely _____ .

5 Fill the space in each sentence by completing the unfinished words.

1 When they went out, they left the baby with a baby-_____ .

2 He was sent home from school because of his punk hair _____ .

3 He put the bottles of milk outside on the door_____ .

4 The houses all collapsed when there was a severe earth_____ .

5 The fire was soon brought under control when a fire-_____ arrived.

6 She lost marks in the test because she had very untidy hand_____ .

7 Large supermarkets have been putting small shop_____ out of business.

8 I sold my second-_____ car and bought a new one.

9 The two cars collided when neither stopped at the cross_____ .

10 I woke up after having a dreadful night_____ .

11 It was raining hard, but luckily my jacket was water_____ .

12 At the end of the wedding, the bride was kissed by the bride_____ .

13 Suddenly I heard foot_____ coming along the corridor.

6 In each space put a word ending in -er(s) -or(s) or -ess.

1 I had this dress made by a _____ my mother knows.

2 I went to the _____ to have my hair cut and set.

3 We bought an electric _____ but it wouldn't fit in the kitchen.

4 She is one of the best known film-_____ in the world.

5 The _____ took our order, but she was a long time bringing it.

6 He was the only _____ of the crash, which killed 50 people.

7 Young people between the ages of 13 and 19 are known as _____ .

8 The football team was loudly cheered by its _____ .

9 On his wall was a large _____ of his favourite singer.

10 The new stadium holds over 100,000 _____ .

11 The central heating works, but this _____ doesn't get hot.

12 The _____ on the bus came up to us and we bought our tickets.

WORD BUILDING (2)

1 Fill the space in each sentence by completing the unfinished words.

1 Waiter, please take this food back. It's under _____.
2 If you fail the exam, you can re-_____ it in December.
3 If you co _____ with us, then we'll get the job finished quicker.
4 They crossed the road by the sub _____ which saved a lot of waiting.
5 He wrote his auto _____ when he had retired from his job.
6 He was very dis _____ with his job, nd decided to resign.
7 This room is for non- _____ ; if you want to smoke, please go outside.
8 She had to work late in the evenings, but they paid her over _____.
9 I went there last Friday and stayed over _____ with an old friend.
10 Will all the ship's passengers please be ready to dis _____.
11 We gave him the prize because his short story was out _____.
12 They dis _____ travelling by bus, so they went by train.
13 He under _____ the word to draw attention to its importance.
14 She couldn't over _____ the bus because the road was too narrow.
15 When you go camping you have to put up with some dis _____.

2 Fill the space in each sentence by completing the unfinished word.

1 The hotel is not respons _____ for anything left in the rooms.
2 The fire started because of her care _____.
3 Her per _____ in the play was praised by the critics.
4 The scar is so small that it's hardly notice _____.
5 He had a very unhappy child _____, which influenced his character.
6 I would verymuch like to have your friend _____.
7 To his amaze _____ the flying saucer landed in his garden.,
8 When he explained the answer to me, I felt very fool _____.
9 They sent me a book _____, explaining how to apply for the university.
10 Every employ _____ in this company receives a bonus at Christmas.

11 The authorities decided to wide _____ the road as it was dangerous.
12 The police praised her hero _____ attempts to rescue the child.
13 The film was considered to be unsuit _____ for children.
14 In add _____ to painting the walls, we also washed the floor.
15 If you pick mushrooms, be careful not to pick the poison _____ kind.

3 In each sentence, make a word to fill the space, using the word given.

1 She _____ took the dinner things back into the kitchen — HURRY
2 I don't buy _____ vegetables, because we have fresh ones. — FREEZE
3 When he gave us the money, I was moved by his _____. — GENEROUS
4 The stamps in my collection have become quite _____. — VALUE
5 The _____ of the sea here must be over 100 metres. — DEEP
6 No-one saw him again after his sudden _____. — APPEAR
7 The company lost money because of bad _____. — MANAGE
8 She couldn't get on with her boss, so gave in her _____. — RESIGN
9 At the interview, they asked him what _____ he had. — QUALIFY
10 The weather changed _____, and they got very wet. — EXPECT
11 She left home and found her own flat, to be more _____. — DEPEND
12 He was not _____ to drinking wine, and quickly got drunk. — CUSTOM
13 There was nothing we could do, so the accident was _____. — AVOID
14 The cashier gave him a _____, after he had paid. — RECEIVE
15 There was a fire next door but our house was _____. — DAMAGE

4 In each sentence, make a word to fill the space, using the word given.

1 The flat had many _____, so we decided not to take it. ADVANTAGE
2 She shouted _____ at the boy to get out of the garden. ANGRY
3 When should I send in my _____ form for the job? APPLY
4 He was very _____, and in the end she agreed. PERSUADE
5 At the moment there is a _____ of fresh vegetables. SHORT
6 Luckily they were _____ in the accident, and walked home. INJURE
7 The jewels I bought turned out to be completely _____. WORTH
8 She felt _____ out after the race, and had to rest. WEAR
9 He left the company after a _____ with his boss. AGREE
10 The hot weather made them feel very _____. SLEEP
11 In the sales, there were great _____ in prices. REDUCE
12 Suddenly they heard the _____ sound of police sirens. MISTAKE
13 We all hope that the problem of _____ will be solved. EMPLOY
14 They were afraid of war, so decided to _____ the army. STRONG

5 In each sentence make a word to fill the space, using the word given.

1 The runway at the airport needs _____. LENGTH
2 The next _____ to Amsterdam leaves at 7.30 tonight. FLY
3 The plane crashed because of the _____ of two engines. FAIL
4 This letter is _____, so please don't show it to anyone. CONFIDENCE
5 She was _____ of her work, and knew it was good. PRIDE

6 I _____ dropped the bowl of soup on the kitchen floor. ACCIDENT
7 There was a small _____ statue above the doorway. WOOD
8 This is the _____ from the shore I have ever swum. FAR
9 The hotel I stayed in was quite _____. LUXURY
10 The container was _____ in shape. CYLINDER
11 She works as a sales _____ for a publishing company. REPRESENT
12 I really _____ with you, but I can't help. SYMPATHY
13 To my _____, the dog began to play a tune on the piano. ASTONISH

6 In each sentence, make a word to fill the space using the word given.

1 Her interest in _____ began when she was given a camera. PHOTOGRAPH
2 The _____ of the race was given a prize by the mayor. WIN
3 His _____ from the team was discussed widely in the press. OMIT
4 The _____ of the paintings was a professional job. THIEF
5 I think you owe me an _____, don't you? EXPLAIN
6 She was responsible for the _____ of the exhibition. ORGANISE
7 Her life _____ were stolen from her mattress by a burglar. SAVE
8 She said that the country needed strong _____. LEAD
9 He was one of the most popular _____ of his time. POLITICS
10 He suffered so much from _____ that he blushed a lot. SHY
11 I was surprised by how _____ he was with a brush. SKILL
12 He had difficulties with English _____. PRONOUNCE

CONNECTORS

This is a very general term used here to include useful words and phrases which introduce clauses.

1 *although, in spite of, despite*
a *Although he fell heavily, he wasn't hurt* (*although* + verb)
b *In spite of falling heavily, he wasn't hurt* (*in spite of* + noun)
   In spite of his heavy fall, ...
c *Despite falling heavily, he wasn't hurt* (*despite* + noun)
   Despite his heavy fall ...

2 *as, since, because*
a *He didn't go to the meeting, as he wasn't interested*
b *He didn't go to the meeting, since he wasn't interested*
c *He didn't go to the meeting, because he wasn't interested*

There is no real difference in meaning.

3 *in order to, so as to, so that*
a *They bought a cow, in order to have fresh milk*
b *They bought a cow, so as to have fresh milk*
c *They bought a cow, so that they could have fresh milk*
The most common negative is *so as not to*:
d *They took raincoats so as not to get wet*
   Note: *in order not to* is also possible.

4 *as if, as though*
a *He speaks as if/as though he knows what he is talking about* (he does)
b *He gives people orders as if he were Napoleon* (he isn't!)

5 *the* (comparative)... *the* (comparative)...
a *The fatter people are, the slower they run*
b *The more tired I am, the more unhappy I become*

6 *except for, apart from*
a *Except for John, everyone arrived on time* (John not included)
b *Apart from John, ...* (John not included)
c *Apart from being late, John was also rude* (= as well as)

7 *while, whereas*
Sue is good at running, while/whereas Jane is good at jumping
This is a formal contrast.

EXERCISES
1 Rewrite each sentence, without changing the meaning, beginning as given.
   1 He got caught in the rain, but he didn't get very wet.
     Despite _____ .
   2 He wanted to talk to her, so he phoned her.
     He phoned her so
     _____ .
   3 Janet was the only one who made any mistakes.
     No-one _____ .
   4 I know you don't like sweets so I won't offer you one.
     Since _____ .
   5 I didn't want to waste time, so I started immediately.
     I started immediately so
     _____ .
   6 If a book is short I read it quickly.
     The shorter _____ .
   7 I won't ask you in, because it's late.
     As _____ .
   8 The only one who knew her phone number was Sam.
     Apart _____ .
   9 In spite of hurting her foot, she managed to climb the mountain.
     Although _____ .
  10 He couldn't repair the radio without a screwdriver.
     In order to _____ .
  11 He appears to need a good meal.
     He looks as _____ .
  12 Although I'm in favour, Sebastian doesn't agree.
     I'm in favour, while
     _____ .
  13 It was raining, but we went there on foot.
     In spite _____ .
  14 The only thing I forgot to buy was the butter.
     I remembered _____ .
  15 Although it was snowing, I went for a long walk.
     It was _____ .

DISCOURSE MARKERS

2 Put an appropriate word or phrase from page 107 into each space.

1 She looks _____ she hasn't slept for a week.
2 He crossed the road _____ have to talk to them.
3 They go everywhere by bus, _____ we always travel by train.
4 The doctor decided not to operate, _____ nothing could be done.
5 _____ there was little hope, she didn't give up.
6 The _____ you walk, the _____ you will get home.
7 She lent me some money _____ I could buy a new bike.
8 He couldn't write the test _____ he hadn't brought his pen.
9 He managed to paint the house _____ the bad weather.
10 _____ of feeling unhappy, she managed to enjoy the party.
11 Apart _____ feeling a bit dizzy, she says she's a lot better.
12 It sounds _____ there's going to be trouble at the demonstration.
13 Cats have a liking for fish, _____ dogs seems to prefer meat.
14 She says she isn't nervous, _____ I think she is a little.
15 _____ he knew the answer, he didn't tell anyone.

These are words and phrases which organise and make clear what we say or write. They help the listener or reader to understand exactly what we mean. Though it would be possible to understand without them, they help a great deal. The meanings of expressions in each section are generally the same, and any differences are made clear in the exercises.

1 *Ordering*
first, (first of all),... secondly,...
thirdly,... next,... then,...
finally,... lastly,... in conclusion,...

2 *Adding and emphasising*
also,... furthermore,...(formal)
moreover,...(formal)
in addition (to this),... as well as this,...
besides this,...

3 *Summing up and giving opinions*
in conclusion,... to sum up,...
personally,...

4 *Giving examples*
for example,... = (e.g.) for instance,...
that is,... = (i.e.)

5 *Showing results*
consequently,... as a result,... thus,...
(formal)

6 *Contrasting*
on the other hand,... in contrast,...
by comparison,...

7 *Concession*
however,... nevertheless,...(formal)
(= although this is true)

8 *Punctuation*
Most of these expressions needs either a full stop, or a semi-colon (;) to come before them, and a comma to follow them.

9 *Formality*
Some expressions above are marked as *formal*; in fact, most uses of all the phrases on this page would be part of well-organised speech, or of writing. (The ones marked are more likely to be found in textbooks or complex argumentative texts; it is not advisable to use such expressions in your own writing at this level.)

EXERCISES

1 Choose the most suitable expression in each sentence.

1 Nowadays, television is one of the most popular forms of entertainment. *In addition to this/However* it provides us with the most recent news.

2 There are many different kinds of programmes on television. *On the other hand/For example* there are sports programmes, children's programmes, and various types of comedy entertainment.

3 Watching television has become the main evening activity in many households. *However/As a result*, many hobbies, such as model-making or dress-making, are not as popular as they used to be.

4 In parts of the USA, there are twenty or more TV channels to choose from. *In comparison/In conclusion*, the four channels available in Britain seem a very narrow choice.

5 Many people feel that television takes up far too much of young people's time. *In contrast/Besides this*, they argue that the quality of the programmes is poor, and that there is too much violence.

2 Fill each space in the text with a suitable expression:

personally	however	for example
as well as this	first of all	in contrast
on the other hand		

Living in a village, rather than in a large city, has a number of advantages. (1)_____ there is plenty of fresh air, and it is easy to buy really fresh food, or grow your own. (2)_____, there is peace and quiet, and less stress than in a city. (3)_____, there are a number of problems involved. (4)_____, if the village is isolated, it may be difficult to find health care, or good education. It is always easy to find work in a city; (5)_____, a village may have only farm-work to offer.
(6)_____, I think I would prefer to live in a village in spite of the problems involved.
(7)_____, this is not possible for me at the moment, as I work in a bank, and I have to live near my work.

3 These sentences make up a short text, but are in the wrong order. Read them carefully, and decide what the correct order should be.

1 Thus motorists will be encouraged to park where there is room, and go into the centre by bus.
2 Besides this, parking becomes more and more difficult, and the roads are blocked by parked cars.
3 Nowadays people prefer to use private cars to travel into the city centre, because it is more convenient.
4 First of all, public transport should be improved and made cheaper.
5 However, there are solutions to these problems, which would improve the quality of life in our cities.
6 In addition to this, free car parks should be built outside the city.
7 As a result, there are traffic jams which block the streets and cause problems for both drivers and pedestrians.

SINGULARS, PLURALS, COUNTABLES AND UNCOUNTABLES

1 Common uncountables

These cannot be made plural with s, and cannot be used with a/an. Here are some examples. See Point 4 below for changes of meaning.

Liquids:	water	Solids:	wood
	milk		stone
	beer		glass

Activities:	dancing	Others:	behaviour
	education		weather
	homework		information
	work		bread
	leisure		furniture
Ideas:	love		news
	happiness		hair
	anger		money
			advice
			luggage

2 Irregular plurals

child–children	foot–feet	self–selves
man–men	knife–knives	shelf–shelves
mouse–mice	wife–wives	half–halves
tooth–teeth	life–lives	loaf–loaves
goose–geese	thief–thieves	wolf–wolves

3 Unchanging plurals

a with plural verb

scissors	scales	goods
binoculars	knickers	lodgings
glasses	pyjamas	savings
pants	tights	stairs
shorts	clothes	wages
trousers		

b with singular verb

maths	physics	billiards
draughts	customs	

4 Problems with countables and uncountables

Changes of meaning:
These are only a few examples of many. Most liquids and solids can be changed to countable by adding a piece of/a bottle of, etc.
e.g. bread = a loaf of bread
water = a glass of water

a *some beer; a beer* = a glass of beer, a bottle of beer

b *some light; a light* = a lamp, or something which gives light

c *some lamb* = the meat; *a lamb* = the animal

d *some experience* = in general; *an experience* = a particular event

e *some paper* = to write on; *a paper* = a newspaper

f *some talk* = conversation, rumour; *a talk* = a lecture

g *some iron* = the metal; *an iron* = for ironing clothes with

EXERCISES

1 Put a/an or nothing in each space.

1 Can you get _____ lemonade in that supermarket?

2 This shelf is _____ glass.

3 We need someone for the job who has _____ experience.

4 The teacher gave them _____ homework to do over the weekend.

5 Do you wear _____ pyjamas in the summer?

6 I'll have _____ chicken with baked potatoes, please.

7 He travelled around the country looking for _____ job.

8 If you go out, can you get me _____ paper?

9 We had _____ good weather when we were there on holiday.

10 He is always asking for _____ advice, but he never accepts it!

11 I burnt my finger on _____ iron when I was a little girl.

12 Do you have _____ information about the times of trains to York?

13 Suddenly I noticed _____ water on the floor.

14 Have we got _____ bread? Or shall I go to the baker's?

15 She looked as if she was made of _____ stone.

16 You have given me _____ great happiness.

2 Put is or are into each space.

1 My hair _____ much too long for summer.

2 Where _____ my new yellow trousers?

3 What _____ the news from Floren

4 The wages here _____ very high.

5 That advice _____ very useful; th very much.

6 He says that maths _____ his favourite subject.
7 My new shorts _____ much too tight; I must have put on weight.
8 The money you wanted _____ on the table by the front door.
9 My clothes _____ all still in the washing machine!
10 Where _____ the scissors I lent you last week?
11 The luggage _____ out in the hall waiting to be brought in.
12 I think the customs _____ on the other side of the airport.
13 The information he gives us _____ always useful.
14 All my life savings _____ hidden in my mattress.
15 The goods you ordered _____ still in the warehouse.

3 Make each part of these sentences plural where possible.

1 The thief took the knife from the shelf.
2 I used the scissors to cut the child's hair.
3 There is no news from the customs about our luggage.
4 A huge wolf attacked the grey goose.
5 For this job you need a lot of experience.
6 He put his wages in his trousers and left.
7 His furniture is made of the best wood.
8 He drank the glass of water and went up the stairs.
9 Education is important; please take my advice.
10 He picked up his paper and started to read.
11 A mouse has sharp teeth and likes cheese.
12 His behaviour was very strange.
13 The weather that day filled everyone with hope.

APPENDIX
USEFUL PHRASES

It is important to use acceptable polite forms during discussions and to use phrases which give you time to think. Try to use as many of these phrases as you can. Your teacher will check that you are using them correctly.

1 Checking meaning

I'm not sure I understand what you mean.
What do you mean exactly?
Do you think you could explain exactly what you mean?
I didn't quite catch that – do you think you could say it again?

2 Agreeing

Yes, that's exactly what I think.
I couldn't agree more.
I agree with you entirely.

3 Disagreeing politely

Yes, I agree, but...
Yes, I agree with you up to a point, but...
Well, I think I would say that...
I'm afraid I can't agree with you on that.
We'll have to agree to differ.

4 Explaining

What I really mean is...
Well, if you ask me, the real point is...
What I'm trying to get at is the fact that...
I don't think you quite understand what I mean.

5 Being uncertain

Well, it's not very clear but I would say that it's a...
I suppose it could be a kind of...
It could be a number of things; for example...
I'm not sure exactly.

6 Giving a personal opinion

In my opinion...
Personally I think that...
Well, for me, the most important thing is...

7 Playing for time

Just a minute, let me have another look.
Let me see now...
Well, it's difficult to say, but I suppose...
It depends how you think about it, doesn't it, but I suppose...

e?

nks